APPIPHANY™

HOW TO SLASH APP DEVELOPMENT COSTS BY 30% OR MORE

KERRY ESSON

 This book is a condensed excerpt from: Appiphany™ From Idea to Multi-Million Dollar Exit. The Business Blueprint to Building an Insanely Successful App From Start to Finish.

All inquiries should be made to appiphany@opsguard.io

Creator: Esson, Kerry

Title: Appiphany™: How To Slash App Development Costs By 30% Or More

ISBN:

978-0-6451865-0-5 (ebook)

978-0-6451865-1-2 (paperback)

Disclaimer

The advice provided in this publication is general advice only. It has been prepared without taking into account your objectives, financial situation or business needs. Before acting on this advice you should consider the appropriateness of the advice, having regard to your own objectives, financial situation and business needs. To the maximum extent permitted by law, the author and publisher disclaim all responsibility and liability to any person, arising directly or indirectly from any person taking or not taking action based on the information in this publication.

INTRODUCTION

Building software can be a daunting task, especially if you're not a developer or technically minded. Yet, people like you tend to have some of the best ideas for apps and have a way of thinking outside the box the insiders can't see. This book has been written to give you a proven blueprint that increases the chances of your app being more successful and guarantees you'll get it built in 30% less time than if you were not to follow it. That 30% time saving directly relates to a 30% cost reduction or more. I have validated this saving time and time again by implementing the process into existing teams at both the startup and enterprise levels.

Everything in this book has stood the challenges of time across multiple industry verticals and emerging technologies. What you're about to discover are the seven steps that make any software development project successful and some of the core business principles of building a financially viable app. This book is for anyone that wants to build any kind of software and monetize it while not having any technical understanding or knowledge of software development. This includes entrepreneurs, product owners, product managers, and non-tech founders.

I will take you on a journey of discovery that will provide you with more understanding and insight than most software owners, or business owners for that matter, ever come to have. You will learn techniques and strategies that will grow your app exponentially and utilize several canvases that can provide you with absolute agility to pivot at any time. The process I outline in this book is part of a more extensive program I call Appiphany™. The entire Appiphany™ process has been developed over two decades. It is the culmination of my experience as a developer, CTO, consultant, and highly successful entrepreneur. I provide a subset of this knowledge in this book, hoping it will help you kick start your journey to success and guarantee you get your Minimum Viable Product built in the most cost-effective way possible.

Thank you for downloading this book and welcoming me on your journey to success. I look forward to hearing your extraordinary success stories and feedback.

1

GAINING CLARITY

Take a moment to imagine you have an idea for an app or software solution that you know will change the game. Something that there is an absolute need for and will improve the lives of hundreds of thousands, or millions, or maybe even billions of people. You may or may not be a developer, but either way, you're fully aware your Solution needs to be built as quickly and efficiently as possible. If you need to entice investors to help develop your Solution, you also know you need something tangible to entice them to invest because the days of investing in mere ideas are all but over. You decide to employ a team of developers (whether internally or via an Agency) to turn your vision into a reality. You get them to give you a quote/estimate, and you expect to get your app delivered for the amount you've been quoted and in the timeframe they estimated. 3-6 months into the development process, you're out of budget and have only half the features promised. You still don't have enough to entice further investment, and you can't get to market with what's been 'delivered'.

. . .

Unfortunately, this story is one I've heard time and time again. I've seen startups fail before they even get a chance to get out of the gates due to this very scenario. I've also seen corporate projects run $100's of millions of dollars over budget and still not deliver what was initially requested or promised. So the question is, how do you avoid this all-too-common scenario?

The answer is so simple I can sum it up in one word; Clarity. Clarity is one of the keys to not only slashing development costs but ensuring efficiency and an exceptional end product that your customers will love and rave about to others. Clarity then is the magic key to slashing your development costs by 30% or more but as simple as that sounds, there is more to it. Like everything in life, there is a process or technique, and if we master that process or technique, we have the keys to unlimited success in that particular area of achievement. Almost every step in this book will lead you down the path of either gaining clarity or maintaining clarity. With clarity, we have massive boosts in efficiency and decreases in cost, delivering a significant part of our cost reduction strategy. Clarity, however, is not gained all at once but rather through a strategic sequence, battle-tested in the real world with several hundred successful software projects.

While clarity may seem like an obvious thing you should have when you're building an app or any piece of software, the reality is most projects don't have enough clarity, or worse, they don't have any clarity at all. This is especially true when outsourcing your development work to an agency, contractor, or freelancer but also rings true for existing in-house development teams. If you, the product owner or client, have this grand vision in your head that you know will change lives and have an amazingly positive impact on the world but are struggling to translate that into something your developers also understand. You will lose a vast amount of time during the development process helping the developer/s gain that understanding or clarity.

The battle-tested Appiphany™ process discussed in this book creates absolute clarity for both you, the Product Owner/Client (so you understand your idea even better than you do now), and the Developer. Unfortunately, most development companies or development teams don't follow this process. If they do, it's still very high level, and it doesn't provide the ultimate clarity either side seeks.

You see, when the Developer and the Product Owner/Client both have absolute clarity, something magical happens; efficiency skyrockets, velocity increases, and costs are reduced. As a result, you end up with a better product, with fewer bugs, at a reduced price. 'Wait, what? Did you say I get a better product with fewer bugs, and I get it cheaper?' Absolutely, but first, you must gain absolute clarity yourself. By being crystal clear in your mind about ALL the facets of your product, market, and user, you're able to communicate your idea much more efficiently.

. . .

You also discover who your market is, why they want/need your product, and of course, the problem they have that your app/software is aiming to solve. The process outlined in this book takes you on a journey of discovery and ensures that your project has the absolute best chance for success. It took 20 years to develop this process, and project after project, it continues to prove itself a success generating machine.

The Product Model

In development terms, we call you the Product Owner, and your journey to greatness begins with you gaining absolute clarity. The best way for you to achieve this is by completing a Product Model Canvas. Some of you may be familiar with Stratgyzers' Business Model Canvas which is a tremendous tool that will help you understand your business in short order. But the Product Model Canvas goes deeper and forces you to start thinking about the most important thing when you're building an app or any piece of software; the User/Customer. One of my favorite mantras from Google's Design team is "Focus on the User, and all else will follow". This single mantra should be, without a doubt, your fundamental guiding star when creating anything you expect someone else to use or love.

The canvas I describe in this book is an adaptation of Stratigyzers' Business Model Canvas and the Lean Business Model Canvas. It consists of 11 blocks, and each focuses on a critical product area that will help you validate your idea. It enables you to understand if your idea will be profitable and clarifies how you intend on solving your customers' ultimate 'why' (problem).

While there are business elements to the Product canvas, we must focus almost entirely on the customer. Of the 11 total blocks, 7 of them focus on the customer and how your Solution will reach them, and only 4 of them are business blocks. These are also important, but we always consider the business blocks after discovering **all** of the customer information. 'But why are we leaving the business blocks until last?' you may be wondering. And that's a great question. We leave the business blocks until last because if we don't have a great customer, market, and product fit, there's not much point trying to figure out how we make the product profitable. The customer simply won't adopt it in the first place. So with all this talk about focussing on the customer, it's no surprise the first block we start with is the Customer Segment.

To create the Product Model Canvas, you will need to divide a large piece of paper (A3 minimum but the larger, the better) or a whiteboard into 11 sections. The easiest way I've found to free draw the model is to start with the horizontal line for the very bottom section and then divide the bottom section into two equal parts as per Figure 1.

Figure 1

Then create your central column, followed by dividing the two sections on either side of this column in half as per Figure 1.1, creating five columns.

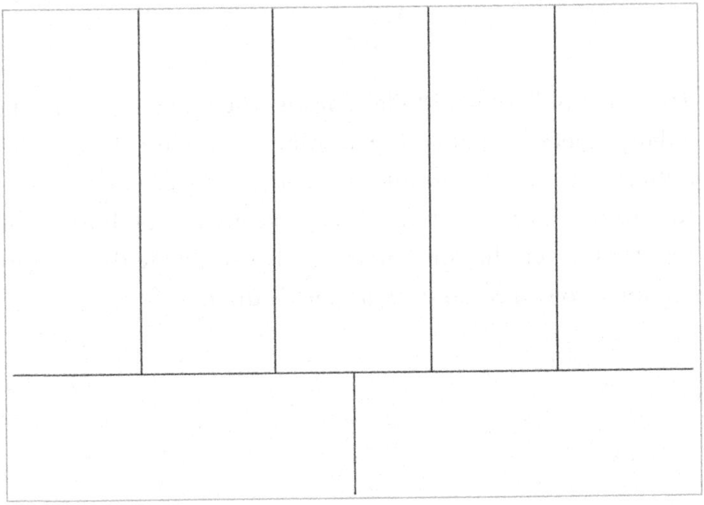

Figure 1.1

All's that's left to do now is draw the horizontal line through columns 2-5 to equally divide the columns into eight separate sections leaving the entire first column open. You will have something that looks like Figure 1.2 once complete.

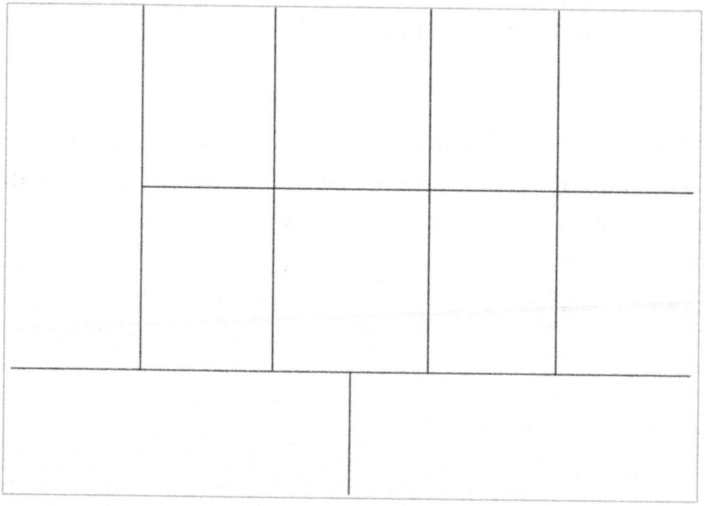

Figure 1.2

Finally, you need to give each of the blocks headings. Working from left to right across the top, we'll start with the first and longest block. Give this the title of 'Customer Segment,' and about halfway down the same block, I want you to add a sub-heading of 'Early Adopter'. In the subsequent block to the top right of Customer Segment, add the title of 'Problem'. Continuing left to right, your next block is 'Value Proposition'. The next block is 'Solution'. The final block in the top right-hand corner is 'Key Success Factors'. Moving down to the second row, the block immediately under 'Problem' is 'Existing Alternatives'. Under the Value Proposition block is 'Channels'. Next is 'Unfair Advantage', and the last block on this row is 'Key Resources and Partners'. Lastly, the two remaining blocks at the bottom are 'Revenue Streams' and 'Cost Structure'. Don't worry about what titles mean for now. I will walk you through the canvas step by step in the coming pages. For the moment, you should have something that looks like Figure 1.3.

You can also download our template from https://go.opsguard.io/appiphany-template-bundle-offer for a small fee, allowing you to print it out on A0 size paper.

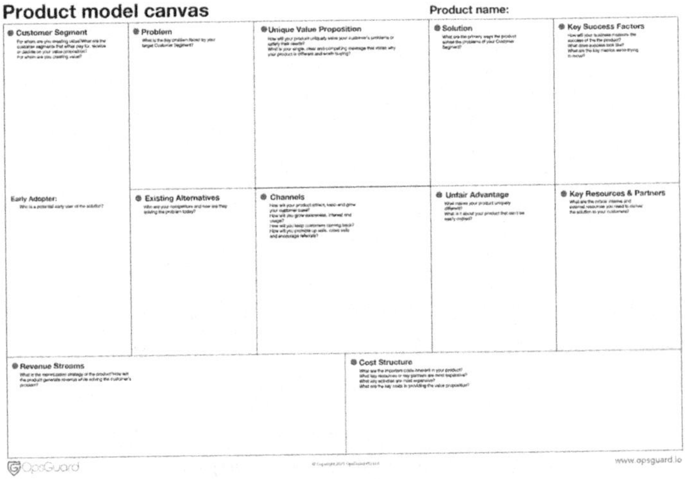

Figure 1.3

If you were to draw an imaginary line down the middle of the canvas, you would see the lefthand side is dedicated entirely to the customer/user. In comparison, the right-hand side is primarily business-related, except for Solution (we'll talk about this a bit later).

Block #1 Customer Segment

As you should know by now, your customer is the most crucial thing your app has. After all, without them, there is no need for you or your great idea in their lives. It is no surprise that the first product area we are faced with is the primary deciding factor in everything else we do with the canvas (and technically the product) moving forward. The customer not only influences the app you're building but also how you will get it into their hands when you're ready.

To understand our customers, we must recreate them and build them up into a Persona, or as some like to call an avatar. This detailed description of your dream client dives into their minds and calls out any pain points, emotions, successes, and failures they may have. You want to understand everything you can about them, so you know exactly how to reach them not just through marketing but also through the design of your software.

Identifying Your Customer Persona

Ideally, we want to use actual customers to model when we complete the Persona but not just any customer. We want the top 4% of our client base, the best customers we have, the dream customers. And we want to take this top 4% and model them on paper to understand how we find others just like them. But using an existing customer base or accessing real customers isn't always possible.

. . .

If you're building a new app, for example, and you don't have any customers yet, you need to look for people you 'think' are your ideal customers. "Easy, I'm my ideal customer," you say. I'm going to tell you right now that you are absolutely not your ideal customer. Even if you believe in your product in your heart of hearts and would buy it in a flash, you're still not your ideal customer. You will always have a cognitive bias towards your product, and in some cases, this can lead to being blind to what your REAL customers want. You will therefore end up with a failed or mediocre performing app. So to avoid this, we need to find an actual customer to model, and the best way to find an actual customer when you have none is to talk to a competitors' customer and model them.

Using a competitors' customer not only provides you some insight into the customers' pain points but also where your competitors' products may not be delivering value. There are many tactics to approach a competitors' customer, but the one I prefer is the least intrusive and also doesn't come across as a sales pitch (because it's not) which is what I like to call the Journalist approach.

With the Journalist approach, you spend the entire time asking questions and gathering information to write a story about later. Like a journalist, you form opinions and gain insight into the person you're interviewing. You're also beginning to build rapport and gain their permission to contact them again later. Now when I say interview, I don't mean inquisition. It should be a simple 10-15 question interview with each question designed to answer our core assumptions the canvas creates and digs ever deeper into understanding what problems the customer has. The whole interview should take no more than 30 minutes, and you should interview no more than ten customers for this exercise. However, between five and seven customers will produce the best results. Research shows that if we interview more than ten people, we start getting the same answers repeatedly, which is great validation, but a waste of our time and resources. You can also do this via a survey if you're struggling to get a meeting with your ideal customer. However, wherever possible, I strongly recommend doing this one-on-one, either in person or via a video chat tool like Zoom or Skype. Of course, you can also use the phone, but I find you build more rapport and get better feedback if you can see one another. It should go without saying, but if the customer can see you, make sure you're professionally dressed, and your surroundings look professional, clean, and tidy.

Again, when choosing the 5-7 customers you're going to interview, they need to be who you think or know to be ***your*** top 4%. If you're a startup or don't have any customers yet, you will need to choose those potential customers you believe will be your ideal customers. If using the Journalist approach with your competitors' customers, ensure you're picking ***your*** ideal customers and not ***their*** ideal customers. It's rather feasible and highly possible your ideal customers are different, or a sub-set, of their customer base, especially if you're a startup on a mission to disrupt an industry.

. . .

To help you form your interview questions, I've compiled a list of sample questions you can use to get started. You can download these from our website for free https://go.opsguard.io/hubfs/Appiphany/Customer-Interview-Questions.pdf. These questions are by no means a comprehensive list. You should adapt and customize these to your industry, product, and most importantly, your core assumption (i.e., the problem you believe your customer has and what your product will be built to solve). It also outlines the interview process and who you should have on your interview team.

Once you've got the data, it's now time to complete the Persona Canvas.

Persona Canvas

The Persona Canvas is your tool to help you build up a picture of your ideal dream customer on paper. Now that you have completed your customer interviews, it should only take 30-90 minutes to complete the canvas in full. It's important to note we're not going to create a Persona for each of the 5-10 customers we interviewed but instead, we're going to aggregate the data into one Persona. We do this because we want a detailed yet broad view of our ideal customer to ensure we want to capture the entire customer segment. There is a caveat, though.

If your product can target vastly different Customer Segments, you should complete a Persona for each, and you should also interview all of these different Customer Segments. For example, this book targets three distinctly different customer segments. The first is entrepreneurs wanting to build a software-based startup, existing Product Owners or Product Managers looking to harness the power of the Appiphany™ process, and finally, anyone who has an excellent idea for an app and needs a third party to develop it for them. Each of these Customer Segments is unique in their motivations, their channels, and to a certain extent, their key reason to buy.

During the interview, you wouldn't (and shouldn't) have asked personal questions of the customer, so you will need to do a little bit of post-interview research to gain some of the demographic info we need for our canvas. The best place to find this info is social media platforms such as LinkedIn, Facebook, and Instagram. These tools give you insight into your customer you otherwise wouldn't have. It only takes five or so minutes per person, so it can be completed in an hour or less. The key areas we are looking to gain some insight into are their average age and their interests. Armed with all this extraordinary knowledge, let's walk through how to complete the canvas. You can download our template from https://go.opsguard.io/appiphany-template-bundle-offer for a small fee.

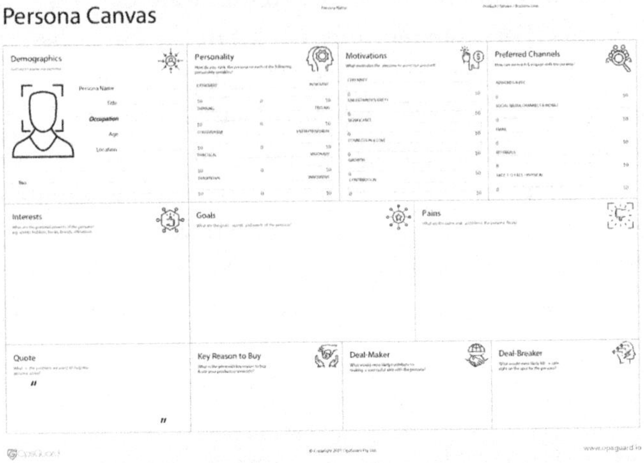

Persona Canvas

Similar to the Product Model, the Persona is broken into 11 blocks, but it doesn't have a set order it needs to be completed in. I prefer to complete the Demographics and Interests first, as these give me a sense of who I'm dealing with when I look at the following three blocks I want to complete (Personality, Motivations, and Preferred Channels).

Completing the Demographics block is pretty straight-forward.

- Start by giving our Persona a name that should allow us to identify their gender (this is only important for marketing and messaging purposes, and if your product isn't gender-specific, it doesn't matter what their name or gender is, as we'll cover this off in our Persona Summary Statement later in this book),

• List their title (if any but it doesn't have to be a corporate title like CEO it could be something that describes your personas daily life such as 'Mom', 'Dad', 'Parent' etc.),

• List their Occupation (again, this doesn't need to be a corporate or work-related title if that doesn't ring true to whom your product is targeted to help, so it could be something like 'Stay at home Mom/Dad'),

• List your Personas age (for the age block, it's recommended you choose an age range such as 18-32, etc. We want an age range as it's doubtful our product will target someone of a specific age but rather an age bracket),

• List their geographic location (usually, this is country or state-based but could be more specific if it needs to be. When it comes to software, rarely would we only want to target people in a specific city unless the software is specific to that city or town (such as a local parking app, for example). However, if our early adopters are in a specific city, we can list this later under the Early Adopters section. Uber and Airbnb are great examples of companies that rolled out their offering to early adopters town by town, targeting specific places and events).

• Now we want to write a short one-sentence bio in the first person (i.e., starting with the word 'I') that gives us a little more insight into our Persona (this is the information we're not going to capture elsewhere such as if they have a university or college degree, if they love pets, have a cat at home, drink red wine, etc. anything that allows us to identify with our Persona better that relates to our product)

• Finally, we want to give our Persona an image or identity to help us relate to them (this can be any random image from the internet that is a good physical representation of our ideal customer/user and matches the demographic info we've just captured)

So now that we've nailed our Persona's Demographics, we want to list out their Interests. They can be anything our Persona has a personal interest in, such as their hobbies, books they like to read, brands they associate with, sports they play, or teams or clubs they affiliate with. Again this kind of information can be garnered from social media channels when completing your post-interview research. The whole point of both the Demographics and Interests blocks is to build our Personas' identity and allow us to relate with them. You can list out as many as you like that are relevant, but 7-10 should be enough. Next, we move to their Personality traits.

When completing the Personality section, we're looking to understand the dominant personality traits our Ideal Customer has. We're not looking for a perfect psychological analysis but rather a guide to help personify our Persona and help us understand what message we may want to use later in our marketing efforts. It can also help us understand how they might be comfortable using our software.

Motivations also help us understand how we might reach our Persona through marketing. More importantly, it tells us the tone we need to present to them in our UI/UX (User Interface/User Experience). It allows us to understand what truly drives them and provides an incredible level of clarity. This section answers the question; "What would be the biggest motivator for me to want to download, use and purchase this software and come back every day?"

This section is one of the most critical parts of the Persona Canvas. I have modeled this section after the six human needs as described by Tony Robbins. If we can unmask which of these needs drives and motivates our customers to use our software, we will reach them in ways our competitors can only dream about. For example, we all need a sense of Certainty in life, yet we also need a level of Variety or Uncertainty. For some people, this can be skewed in either direction, but we always need both. In fact, of the six, we all **need** the first four to some degree as a basic human need, while the last two allow us to gain a sense of fulfillment.

While the titles of the needs are reasonably self-explanatory, the following is a quick summary of each;

• Certainty - This is one of the four basic needs. Certainty crops up in all areas of our life. We need to feel a sense of certainty around things like our finances, a roof over our head, our relationships, and in general ourselves.

• Uncertainty/Variety - Another of the four basic needs. Uncertainty or Variety is critical to ensure we aren't getting bored in our lives. Generally, we need variety in things like the food we eat, where we go on holiday and our friends to name a few.

- Significance - Another of the four basic needs. To some extent, we all need to feel significant. Some people will express this through their physical appearance (such as how they wear their hair, how they dress, or through other physical representations such as a lot of piercings or tattoos, etc.). Others will express this through their actions towards other people by making them feel insignificant or wanting to feel like the most important person in the room.

- Love/Connection - Another of the four basic needs. We all need to feel love and connection to others, whether with our partner, friends, family, or just the people we interact with daily. Some people will express this through affection, and others might express this through their actions.

- Growth - To feel truly fulfilled in life, we need to feel a sense of growth or feel like we are becoming better people, whether physically, mentally, spiritually, or financially, etc. While not a basic need, growth is a great motivator to tap into as it allows people to gain a sense of achievement within themselves.

- Contribution - Another big motivator towards feeling total fulfillment in life is contribution. This is all about giving something back and expecting nothing in return. It could be things like sharing knowledge without reward or donating to charity. Those that contribute will be motivated by something that enables their contribution with ease.

When we focus on our product, we need to ask ourselves which of these six motivators will be most important to our Persona and provide them with a need to come back and use our software ALL the time? If you're building a dating app, for example, Connection & Love would be at the top, followed by Variety and Significance. If you're building a Fintech app, it could that Certainty, Growth, and Significance are dominant motivators. Take the time to really think about which of these are crucial to your product because I promise you if you nail this, you will create raving fans that won't be able to get enough of your software, and you'll blow your competitors entirely out of the water. Once you've completed this, you should know the top three motivators that will drive the UI/UX of your software and marketing messaging. I cannot stress enough just how powerful this is. Just imagine being able to draw your users to your app like a magnet.

The Preferred Channels section is something we will use later in our discovery and will translate to the Channels block in our Product Model Canvas, but for now, answer the following questions; How could I reach my customer? Where do they hang out online? How would I get my app into their hands? Would they spend most of their time on Facebook, Instagram, TikTok, Twitter, Google, LinkedIn, etc.? Think in detail about how and where you can reach your ideal customer.

Now that we've completed the top of the Persona Canvas, we move to Goals and Pains. For our Persona's Goals, we want to ask the following; What is the ultimate outcome we expect our Persona to achieve by using our app? For example, a goal might be; Jane wants to access files anywhere, anytime. Or, Jane wants an easy way to collaborate with customers' documents digitally without them needing to download software.

Once we have listed all of our goals, we then want to list the pains the Persona has. These should be the exact negatives of the goals we just listed. If you think of a Goal or a Pain that doesn't have an opponent in either box, you should list one. In other words, every goal should have a corresponding pain and vice versa. Write as many goals and pains as possible to ensure you gain comprehensive insight and clarity. Your software will need to solve all of their pains and allow them to achieve all of their goals.

We're now beginning to form a great picture of our Persona, and we're ready to move onto the Quote section. The Quote section is the second most crucial part of the entire Persona Canvas. This one block alone is essentially the reason your app/software exists. Your Quote needs to be a single sentence that enables them to achieve ALL of their Goals and alleviate ALL of their Pains. Let's say you're building the first version of Dropbox. Your Quote might be something like, "I have no way to easily store, collaborate and share files with someone that can be accessed anywhere, at any time, by anyone I choose regardless of the platform they choose to use." Powerful stuff, right? This single statement tells me precisely what I need to do to solve this persons' problems and give them an experience they will rave about to others.

. . .

Next, we want to understand their Key Reason to Buy. Simply put, this is your customer's why and their primary reason to purchase your app. What you list here will form part of the Solution block on your Product Model Canvas, but for the purpose of the Persona, we need to answer the following; What is the specific reason this Persona would want to use my app/software? What precisely does this solve? How does this app/software make their life better?

Phew, we are almost done! Before we tackle the last two sections, let's quickly recap what we now understand about our ideal customer. We know enough about their demographics that we're able to target them. We know their interests and their motivators, which describes our UI/UX and marketing tone. We know the type of personality they might have and how we might reach and interact with them. We also know what interests them and their goals and pain points. We understand ***why*** they want to buy from us and their ultimate problem statement (Quote). The final things we want to know are the things that would sell them on the spot and the things that would send them running for the hills before they buy from us.

The Deal Maker section is your opportunity to identify your app or software's key buying points (or buying reasons). It needs to include intangibles (or in software terms 'non-functionals') like; "It's easy to use and understand," "It doesn't matter what device I have, it works," or "It's always there when I need it". It could also include things like; "no lock-in contract", "no upfront cost" or, "it's free unless I need XYZ feature". The primary question you need to answer here is;

What would most likely contribute to making a successful sale with the Persona? Don't hold back. You want to take this opportunity to blow your competition out of the water. Why are you better? What entices them to use your product or service over your competitor?

Finally, we move to our last block, which describes our Deal Breakers. These will most likely be the opposites of what you've just listed as your Deal Makers. But may also include additional items such as poor communication, poor customer service, poor reviews, or anything else that might destroy your chances of winning and retaining that customer. Make sure you list all you can think of, as these will be used later to ensure you have the systems and processes in place to avoid your customer ever experiencing a Deal Breaker moment.

Well done! You now understand your potential customer better than most entrepreneurs or intrapreneurs ever do. In addition, you are better positioned than most to build an app or piece of software that will attract users on mass and create raving fans. But what you may not have yet realized is you've just created a whole lot of assumptions about your dream customer that, later in this book, we look to validate. You've made assumptions about their motivations, how to reach them, their goals and pain points, their key reason to want to buy from you, and the holy grail of all assumptions, their ultimate problem statement. The pivotal point to take away is that we must validate our assumptions and be willing to adjust them later once we have authentic user feedback. Later in this book, I provide a simple process that enables you to adapt or pivot your product model if your assumptions aren't stacking up.

Before we transfer this information onto the Customer Segment Block, I want to discuss the assumptions register briefly. An assumptions register is a list of all of the assumptions we will form throughout the Appiphany™ process. It's a vital part of being successful as it captures everything you assume to be correct and prompts you to validate this throughout your journey. I discuss this in-depth in the Customer Validation chapter, but for the moment, create a simple table or spreadsheet and list all of the assumptions you have made thus far, and any more we form as we continue through the process.

The final step is to transfer all of this fantastic information onto the Customer Segment Block of our Product Model Canvas in the form of a Persona Statement. Your Persona Statement is simply a paragraph that sums up your entire Persona Canvas and makes it easy for anyone reading it to identify and connect with your target market. An example of an excellent Persona Statement might be; "The primary Client is aged between 20-30 and situated within the lower to middle class. They are highly motivated by growth, certainty, and a sense of significance and prefer digital means of engagement and communication. They have a strong word-of-mouth culture and will generally follow the status quo if they see others succeed. The problems they face are the lack of financial intelligence associated with managing wealth, the lack of not having anyone to trust or help them with their financial problems, the feeling of helplessness and lack of control, and the lack of financial direction. They are excited by homeownership, travel, building a family, a sense of security, and feeling like they are accepted and living with purpose. They are motivated to use the app due to transparency, education, and automation but would be demotivated to use the app due to a lack of trust or security, being too costly, receives negative reviews or the apparent lack of value."

Can you see how this statement considers the entire Persona and clearly defines whom you're targeting? This is super powerful! Anyone can read this and understand exactly who you're targeting, how to reach them, and why you're targeting them. I can tell you right now, over the last 20 years of consulting, less than 2% of everyone I've dealt with could provide you with this level of understanding of their customer. Yet everyone in your organization from, your CEO to your call center staff, MUST have this level of insight to truly connect with your customer. You have just uncovered one of the most empowering facets of a successful business and now have a leg up on 98% of other companies. Well done!!

Identify your early adopter

Now that we know what our dream buyer looks like, we want to identify a subset of this buyer group that would likely be our early adopters. Early adopters can be defined as customers that are most likely to take your app onboard first and be more patient with tiny early day bugs. They will almost always be more tech-savvy than the rest and, therefore, most likely sit in the lower age bracket of your Persona. Identifying our early adopters then is simply a matter of refining our Customer Persona a smidge more. As a general rule, the only thing that should be adjusted when looking at your early adopter is the Demographics of the Persona you just created. There may be tweaks in Interests, Personality, Motivations, and Preferred Channels, but the rest of the canvas should remain unchanged. You want to refine your Persona a little further to know who you want to target later with your Minimum Viable Product (MVP).

Similar to our Persona Statement, we also want to create one for our Early Adopter. A follow-on example for the Persona Statement we created above might be; "22-25-year-olds living Melbourne Australia with interests in Investment Banking, Insurance, Credit Cards, Entrepreneurship, Investing, Business, and Online Banking or Management. They are either at university, a graduate, a postgraduate, or have a professional or post-doctorate degree. They are generally working in legal services, sales, business, finance, management, architecture, engineering or life, physical and social sciences." You will note this statement zeroes in on fine-tuning the demographics and nothing more.

Block #2 Problem

Given the incredible Customer Persona you've just completed, you already know all of your customer problems. You know their ultimate problem statement, which captures the essence of the problem you're trying to resolve, or in other words, the cause. Being aware of the cause is crucial because it is your customers' ultimate 'why'. The reason they have the problem and the reason they will pay you to fix it.

So we simply need to transfer your Persona's ultimate problem statement (Quote) in the Problem block, and we're ready to move on to the next section.

Block #3 Solution

It could be argued that the Solution is defined by a tangible outcome (something you can physically deliver (virtual or otherwise) to the customer) which means it's a business-related block. I would, however, argue the Solution is both a business-related block AND a customer-related block because it is both a tangible outcome and the Solution to the customers' problem.

The Solution is the primary way/s your product solves the ultimate problem statement of your already defined Customer Segment. The fastest way for you to define your solution statement is to list all of the dot points that counteract the pains/problems your customer has. You then turn these dot points into a single statement that defines how you solve the problem/s.

Following on from the Dropbox problem statement we defined when completing our persona canvas; "I have no way to easily store, collaborate and share files with someone that can be accessed anywhere at any time by anyone I choose regardless of the platform they choose to use".

. . .

Your solution statement might read something like, "A cloud-based file repository that allows a user to easily store, collaborate and share files with anyone, regardless of time, place, or platform". How powerful is that statement? If anyone asks you what you do or your elevator pitch, you now have an obvious and to-the-point message.

Okay, so we now know who we're targeting, their problem, and how we intend to solve it. It's now time to consider our competition.

Block # 4 Existing Alternatives

To put it simply, your Existing Alternatives are all of the Competitors your dream clients are currently working with. If you haven't done competitor research yet, I'm so glad you're reading this BEFORE building your app/software. Almost all software will have market competition to some degree. It's very rare these days to have a unique idea for an application or piece of software. The exception to this rule is with regards to emerging technologies such as blockchain and artificial intelligence, although this gap is closing very fast. The next prominent movement will be when quantum computing technologies merge into the mainstream.

Conducting competitor research is crucial to the success of your business, let alone the software you're building. You need to have a crystal clear view of the market you're aiming to play in. When we conduct Appiphany™ workshops with our clients, we expect they have already completed this process by following the pre-workshop training we provide. If you've already completed a competitor analysis, you can still follow the methodology outlined in this chapter and compare the two. You may end up learning even more about your competitors.

To conduct a competitor analysis, we're going to utilize another canvas. You may be starting to wonder why we use so many canvas's, and the answer is because they focus only on the things that really matter and ignores everything else. They also make it easy for us to visualize the specific area we're concentrating on. Furthermore, a canvas is something you can use to quickly pivot or monitor an old idea or assess a new idea.

The methodology I outline here has two components. It is by no means going to give you an in-depth view. However, it will provide you with enough information to understand the competitive landscape to a level that will ensure you know who they are, what they offer, and how you can succeed in providing a solution that will leave them wondering how they missed seeing you coming.

We're going to begin by listing all of the competitors we can find. Some of these we may have already discovered when we completed our Persona Canvas, and others we may need to do a little research to find out who they are. I like to list ALL competitors to my business, even if they only offer part of what I do. I prefer this approach because I want to know everyone I need to be better than and not just my top 5 or 10 competitors. In the world of innovation, any of these competitors could emerge as my number one in a very short time, so I want to be prepared to combat them if they do. Once we've listed all the competitors we can find, it's now time to utilize the Competitor Analysis Canvas.

Competitor Analysis Canvas

The Competitor Analysis Canvas is made up of 7 Blocks and is designed to give you a quick snapshot of a particular competitor and their offering/s. You should complete one of these for every competitor you've already identified. If a specific competitor has more than one product that competes with you, you should also complete a canvas for each of these competing products. You'll note that 5 of the 7 blocks ask for an individual score which we use later to find the Total Competitor Score. You can download our template from https://go.opsguard.io/appiphany-template-bundle-offer for a small fee.

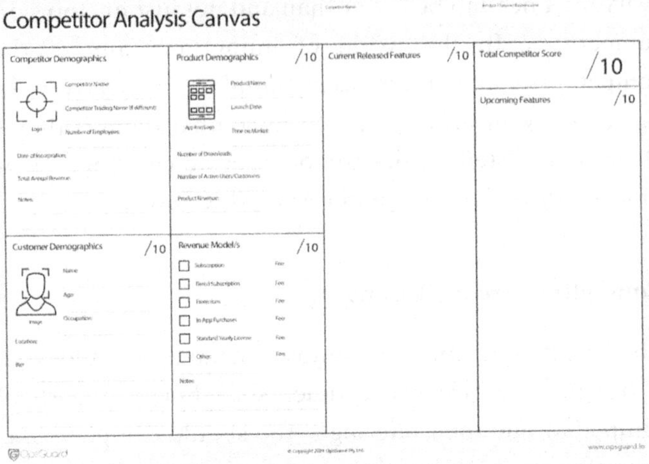

Competitor Analysis Canvas

To begin, we complete the Competitor Demographics section. This is very straightforward and lets us know the name of the competitor we're dealing with, the number of employees they have, when they started in business, and their annual revenue. This allows us to quickly identify the scale of the competitor, which in turn enables us to formulate a plan to win customers away from them later. For example, the way we approach large multinational corporate customers will be very different from how we approach small startup customers. If the company is public, you will easily garnish this information, but if it's not, you may not be able to gather accurate numbers. A great source of this type of non-listed company data can be found on LinkedIn, Crunchbase, and Glassdoor.

We now move on to the Customer Demographics section. There is a good chance this will be identical to what you've already done in your Persona Canvas. If so, you can copy this info across, but this may not always be true. For example, you may be targeting a more specific subset of a competitors' customer base that you know they are under servicing. An example would be identifying a competitor with a cookie-cutter approach and a one-size-fits-all offering. You might decide to target a younger demographic with a more dynamic and tailored offering. In this case, you want to list the demographic you believe most of your competitors' revenue is generated from and not the specific subset demographic you intend on targeting. Once you've completed this section, give it a score out of 10, with ten being identical to your Customer Demographics and one being completely different.

Next, we move to the Product Demographics section. This details all of the vital information we need to know about a competitors' product. To begin, write down the name of the product. In some cases, a company may have only one product, and the Product Name and Company Name are the same. If this is the case, write in the company name once again. The details we want to know about the product are:

- Its launch date.
- Time on the market as of today.
- The number of downloads or installs.
- The number of active users/customers.
- The revenue or estimated revenue from this product.

Again this info can be hard to find but is invaluable to you as an emerging competitor. I recommend using App Annie to garnish most of this data. Now give this section a score out of 10, with ten being much higher than your 12-month projections and one being much lower.

After understanding the high-level details of the product, we now want to gain a detailed understanding of the features and functions of your competitors' offerings. You can use this detail later to complete a feature comparison, but for now, it lets you see where you stand as far as what you're offering customers in comparison. List all the features your competitors' app has. Most of this will publicly available on their website, but if you can, download the app and use it yourself. This is a great way to understand what you're up against. Once again, we want to give this section a score out of 10, with ten being identical to your go-live features and one being very different.

Now that we understand all of the current features, we want to know what they have coming soon and what's further in the pipeline. Most software providers make this information available on their website for their customers' benefit, but it's also valuable for competitors. If they don't publicly list it, do some digging on their support portals and forums and see what the most requested features are. If you can offer this functionality before your competitor, you'll go a long way in winning your potential customers' business. This section also requires a score out of 10, but we're going to score this a little differently. If you have all of the same features in your future backlog AND have none of them in your go-live list, then you will score this section a ten (because your competitor is more competitive in this instance). For every feature you have in your go-live list, you can reduce the score, BUT if they have valuable features in the pipeline you don't, you increase the score again as once more, their product might be more competitive than yours. Essentially, you want to gauge whether you are more competitive from day one or less competitive with your proposed upcoming features. When we think about it, this is the future vision your competitor has for their product, so are you exceeding their offering, matching it, or are they going to outperform you in the long run?

Once we have all of the current and future features listed, we now complete the Revenue Model section. The Revenue Model section tells you how your competitor is monetizing their offering, what type of revenue model your customers are familiar with, and how much they're charging your potential customers. This section is pure gold as it helps you know where to set your pricing and the type of revenue model your customer is comfortable engaging with. Again, score this section out of 10, with ten being identical to your intended revenue model and pricing and one being very different.

Great job!! You've almost completed your first competitor analysis. The last thing we want to do is add all of the out of 10 scores we've listed and divide it by five to get the average. This is your Total Competitor Score. The higher the number, the bigger a competitor they will be, either from day one, or in the near future. The scoring model is a little subjective, but it's a simple way to quickly see who your real competitors are. If they're offering an identical product to identical customers with identical revenue models and fees, then they are, without a doubt, your biggest competitor. Now you need to figure out how to surpass them and make your offering exceed your customer expectations, all while creating raving fans. This then leads us to Block #5, Your Unfair Advantage.

Block #5 Your Unfair Advantage

If you've made it this far then, a big congratulations is in order. You've garnished more insight and clarity in the last 20 odd pages than most businesses learn in a lifetime. While we're not quite halfway with the blocks as yet, I promise this process starts to speed up as we've begun to gather some of the information already, and the following three blocks benefit from this.

Your unfair advantage is your secret sauce. Your magic that customers love over your competitors and the key thing that drives them to you while helping create raving fans. Your Unfair Advantage should be difficult for your competitors to replicate quickly and should be able to stand the tests of time. This doesn't mean it's locked in stone and can't be flexible or pivot if needed. Everything we've done thus far must be flexible or agile. We need to have the ability to adjust and move with our market, our customers' desires, and of course our competitors.

To understand Your Unfair Advantage, you first need to understand your reason for wanting to either be in business or build this product in the first place. You had to see a need in the market for what you're offering and knew you could deliver a better solution. If your idea is not unique and you have competitors you're copying, then the trick is to identify the gaps they have in the market. To do this, consider asking the following questions;

- What segment of the market are they under servicing and why?

- What features are they lacking that I could build instead?

- How good is their UI/UX, and could I significantly improve a users' experience by offering an outstanding design?

- What price point have they set their product at, and could I offer my product at a higher or lower price to better appeal to my target customer?

- Which of the six human needs is the biggest motivator of my target customer, and are my competitors serving these adequately?

Unfortunately, I can't tell you what Your Unfair Advantage is. You need to figure that out on your own, but I can help you find what it is by answering the questions above and reminding you what your reason for doing this was in the first place. You would have gained a lot of insight already through your customer interviews that you conducted when completing your Customer Persona. If you're unsure and are absolutely stuck, go back and ask your competitors' customers this question 'If a new product entered the market, what would it need to be, or do that would convince you to change over?' You will get various responses, but I can almost guarantee there will be a few common ones.

1. Migration - given we're talking about someone committing to change software, migration will be a common theme that will cause them to want to stay where they are. Moving and migrating existing data can be problematic, time-consuming, and costly. So consider this when you design your product so you can move someone to your platform quickly and with little stress or effort on their part.

2. Lack of features - In general, someone isn't going to move if you lack feature parody. Now that doesn't mean you must have 'all' of the features your competitors do, but you must have all of the features your customer utilizes or needs. There is a crucial distinction there, which is even more true if you're looking to disrupt an industry with established players. In this instance, there's a good chance your competitors are over-servicing these customers, which means their product is more expensive than it needs to be.

3. Cost - I've deliberately left this until last because many new businesses think they need to be cheaper than their competitors to gain market traction. But this is only true in some cases. I've found that more often than not, if I increase the price of my product, more people will buy it. Why? Because people see more value in a product that has a higher price. However, we need to be logical and assess each product, its ideal customer, and its market before deciding the price point. In the example of a disruptor moving into an established market and targeting an over serviced customer segment, your price is going to be cheaper, which is precisely what they're looking for. Alternatively, you might offer more features at the same price as your competitors.

Again your customer sees more value in your offering because they get more for the same price. You might note the common theme here that your price point is entirely related to the value your customer perceives in your product.

When you see your Unfair Advantage written, it should inspire you, excite you and provide you with absolute certainty that your product is better than anyone else in the marketplace. Remember, this is the crucial thing that sets you apart from your competitors and something difficult for them to replicate quickly. If we continue with the first version Dropbox analogy, I used earlier in this book. Your Unfair Advantage might read something like, "We provide secure, digital access to files anytime, anywhere without the need to own costly infrastructure or pay costly technicians". You will note this closely aligns with the customer Quote we wrote in our Persona. And at the time, low-cost cloud-based file management didn't exist. You needed to manage your own costly servers, which meant not just the cost of the servers, electricity, and cooling but the cost of staff to run and maintain them. It was Dropbox's secret sauce at the time and the key market differentiator.

Block # 6 Unique Value Proposition

Some people confuse the Unfair Advantage block and the Unique Value Proposition (UVP) block. Your Unfair Advantage is what makes you different from your **competitors**, whereas your UVP is the essence of the value you provide your customers and confirms your product and customer fit. In other words, it's "why your product uniquely solves your customers' problems and satisfies their needs". It's the thing that makes them raving fans and long-term customers. It's their main reason to buy, meets all of their goals, and solves all of their pain points, as well as being the thing that keeps them coming back time and time again.

This all might be sounding a little familiar as you will begin to recall the Key Reason to Buy (Deal Makers), Goals, and Pain Points were all things we discovered when we completed our Customer Persona. We also highlighted the Persona's problem statement in their Quote. All of these things combined provide us with our Unique Value Proposition. What's left for us to do is sum it all up in a one, or two-sentence statement. Suppose we continue to utilize the Dropbox example we've used throughout the canvas so far. Our Unique Value Proposition statement might look something like this; "We are the first to offer someone a low-cost way to easily store, collaborate and share their files with anyone they choose that can be accessed anywhere at any time regardless of the platform they choose to use. All while providing a simple and easy to use user interface while ensuring our application servers are always available". In that single statement, you solve all of the customers' problems, remove all of their pains and ensure you meet their Deal Makers and avoid their Deal Breakers. That is your Unique Value Proposition.

Block #7 Channels

The Channels block is going to be a very quick one to do as you've already identified this information when you completed your Customer Persona. The only difference is we want to be more specific and list out the Social Media or Ad platforms etc. we intend to use to reach our target audience. We want to list precisely where our Customer segment hangs out online, so when the time comes to market to them, we know exactly where we're targeting them. This also provides us with a sense of what our Cost Per Lead (CPL) and Cost Per Acquisition (CPA) might be, but I touch more on these metrics in the next section.

Take the time to write specifically where your customers can be found based on the order of preference you identified in your Persona Canvas.

Block #8 Key Success Factors

Welcome to your first business block. The Key Success Factors are your measures for understanding whether your app/software is achieving the desired level of success. These are the specific measures that tell you immediately if your app is being successful or failing. Everything your business does should be measured. Otherwise, your risk of failure dramatically increases. You may be familiar with the term Key Performance Indicators (KPIs), and that's what this block is all about. We need to set the indicators that we can track and measure to know if our app is performing as well as we might expect. For example, if we're not getting downloads, then we need to investigate why that is and correct it.

From a software perspective, our KPIs are usually measured in the form of downloads, the total number of active users, and revenue generated. If any of these things are lacking, we may be in for some trouble down the road. All KPIs should be tracked, measured, and reviewed regularly; otherwise, the task we're about to undertake in setting them is a waste of time.

The additional metrics we will want to track are our marketing metrics. These tell us how successful our marketing campaigns are and if the channels we've chosen are accurate. The three main ones are Cost Per Lead (CPL), Average Cost Per Acquisition (ACPA), and Lifetime Customer Value (LCV). The CPL tells us how much it cost to turn a cold prospect into a lead. Different businesses treat leads differently, but in software, a prospect normally becomes a lead when they download or sign up for a free trial. ACPA tells us how much in total we have to spent to turn that lead into a paying customer. LCV tells us how much a customer is worth to the company over the entire period we expect them to be customers.

The first KPI we are going to track is the number of downloads/installs. This is the number of times our app or software has been downloaded from an app marketplace or our own server and installed on a device. If your app is a web application and therefore not downloadable, we're going to track the number of accounts created or signups. These are the first engagement we have with a new user, so this is the first thing we want to track. This may also be when someone becomes a lead.

. . .

The subsequent KPI is the number of active users. The definition of an active user can vary depending on who you ask or the type of app you have. The deciding factor should come down to the regularity you expect your users to be logged in and using your app or physically gaining a benefit from it. If you expect your users should be logging in daily, then it's the daily number of active users. If you expect them to log in a few times a week, then it's the weekly number of active users, or if they only need to log in a few times a month, then it's the monthly active users. If you're unsure where to start, I suggest starting with weekly or monthly, but the additional variable we haven't discussed yet is your revenue model/s.

The third KPI you need to track is your revenue model/s. We discuss the different types of revenue models in detail in Block 10, but for now, these are the main ones to consider; Subscription, Freemium, In-App Advertising, In-App Purchases, and Data Monetization. Your app can and should utilize more than one of these revenue models.

Downloads, Registrations & Installs

Tracking the number of times a user downloads, registers for, or installs your application is a key metric to understand the effectiveness of your marketing efforts and therefore guides you on which campaigns are achieving more significant value. We also want to compare this metric with the number of active users to gauge our attrition rate (the number of users we lose or are 'dead' accounts). From a Cost Per Lead (CPL) perspective, we want to know how much it cost us to get the user to this point.

. . .

The way you track this metric can be achieved in multiple ways depending on how your user accesses your software. If they download the software from your website, for example, you have several means to track their downloads, with the smartest and most valuable being capturing their email address. If your app is installed via Google Play or Apple AppStore, both of these provide detailed install and uninstall data. If you have a web app, tracking registrations is as simple as tracking downloads from a website by utilizing a user's unique email address. Regardless of how the user first installs your application, we must also be tracking where they came from and what it cost to get them there. Google Analytics is an excellent tool for tracking where leads have come from and what Google charged to get them there. Facebook also gives you details on the costs to gain leads. Combining these tools with an excellent Marketing intelligence platform such as HubSpot allows you to generate these numbers effortlessly.

There are also plenty of other third-party software solutions that will give you detailed metrics and tracking data, including App Annie, AppTweak, Flurry, and Appfigures, to name a few. Most of these will track all three of our key metrics as well as our CPL and ACPA.

Active Users

The Active Users KPI allows us to understand the health of our business, and if our app is providing the value we expect it to. If users are downloading the app and then not engaging with it, or worse, uninstalling it/canceling their registration, we have a real problem we need to solve. The issues are either we have missed the mark entirely with our Customer Problem assumption, or we have a significant issue with our UI/UX. Discovering which of these is the cause of a high attrition rate will be the critical factor in the success of your software. After all, the more users you retain, the more successful your software and business will be.

Defining what constitutes an active user can make or break your business. You need to take this metric seriously and be firm with the parameters that constitute an active user.

Part of active user tracking is the conversion of trial customers to paying customers and retaining those users for at least 12 months. This allows us to understand what our Cost Per Acquisition is. We use Average Cost Per Acquisition rather than Cost Per Acquisition is because the cost to acquire a single user can fluctuate. Therefore, we want to track the average over time and work as hard as possible to bring the cost of this number down.

Tracking Revenues

Tracking revenues is the simplest of the three metrics. All subscription and accounting platforms will track your revenue for you. What they won't track or calculate easily is your Lifetime Customer Value (LCV). Simply put, this is the total amount of revenue you can expect to receive from a customer over the entire time they are with you. To calculate your LCV, you need to multiply the average monthly revenue by the maximum number of months they can be a customer. If your business is new, you will typically only consider the lifetime of a customer 12 months. As your business ages, you can increase the timeframe to reflect what the data tells you.

Block # 9 Key Resources & Partners

Block 9 is all about identifying who you need to work with and the resources you need to get the software into the hands of your users. Your Key Resources are anything that needs to contribute to you being able to reach and deliver your value proposition. It will include things like;

- Financial resources - the ability to have the financial means to build and maintain your software and market it to your Customer Segment, specifically your Early Adopters. Whether you're building the app in-house or through an agency, you have a physical, financial cost. You also need to be able to afford to reach your customers and make them aware your app exists. The more funds you have for marketing, the faster your user base will grow. When I speak to many founders, they are focused on raising capital to build their awesome app. Very few realize they also need the funds to market to their Early Adopters as, without user growth, further investment is challenging, and you'll be giving away more equity than you need to. The moral of the story, always raise capital for both the initial build AND marketing to your initial user base.

- Human resources - These are the talented people you need to build, maintain and market your app. You also need people to support your customer base to enable you to provide exceptional customer service. Remember, one of our guiding Mantras is "focus on the user, and all else will follow." So you need to make sure once you get your customers on board, you keep them through, not just an exceptional product but exceptional customer service. Generally, your customer won't contact you after the point of sale unless something has gone wrong or they have questions. So you need to ensure you have the support in place to excite and blow these people out of the water. These are the people that become raving fans. But your goal should be to make all of your users raving fans by offering them more value than your competitors.

• Infrastructure - all software will need some kind of Infrastructure to run on, and unless you're building a desktop app, you're going to require servers to support your backend or the brains of your software. These days, cloud computing is the norm, so your backend will most likely live in the cloud. Building mobile apps is not always the best option, especially when people have so many apps on their phones. It may be better to offer a mobile responsive web app, which means your front end will also be in the cloud. Either way, you will need both the physical resource of the cloud provider and the human resource to support and monitor it.

• Time - Not a common thing we as humans tend to think of as a resource but time is a critical resource when you're building software. You need to ensure you give yourself enough time to develop your app. There is no point in creating something you have to burn to the ground later because it was built without consideration for testing and documentation. Most agencies fail here as they want you in and out as fast as possible so they can move on to the next client. Whenever you work with an agency, you must mandate both automated and physical testing and solid documentation. I touch more on this later in the Selecting Your Developer section, but I want to seed the idea now that super fast is not always good. There are exceptions, but as a general rule, you want time to give your software the respect it deserves as your users will thank you for it.

Partners are those organizations or external resources we need to ensure we deliver our value proposition. They can be any or all of the Human resources and Infrastructure I mentioned above. They can include;

- Development Agency
- Cloud Service Provider
- Managed Cloud Service Provider
- Marketing Agency
- External Customer Support Agency
- Accountants
- Lawyers
- Investors
- Shareholders
- and more...

Partners can also be other organizations with a nonconflicting product that already has your ideal customer base. These are excellent growth tools, and the cost of acquiring customers in these kinds of partnerships is nearly always much less than traditional marketing. Take the time to list out any possible partners you may be able to do a joint venture with. These are gold when you're an early-stage startup or have a new product as they introduce you to your customer segment without the same level of marketing costs. Furthermore, they're a warm lead, and warm introduction, meaning your conversions can be as high as 70-80%.

Block #10 Revenue Streams

I could write an entire book on the different revenue models you could use to generate income from your software, but for this book, I'll focus on the main ones and give you an explanation of each with the pros and cons.

Subscription Model

Traditionally, the subscription model was the norm in software. Microsoft was one of the pioneers of this model, and it's still one of their key revenue generators today. The subscription model depends on your user paying you a monthly, quarterly, or yearly fee in return for the use of your software. Generally, this will include all updates and features released within that period. The most widespread structure with the subscription model is as follows;

1. Free 7, 14, or 30-day trial (generally, this is the full version of the software)

2. Monthly Subscription (costs more than yearly); and

3. Yearly Subscription (usually billed with the incentive of one or two months free)

Pros

1. By incentivizing your annual plan, you usually get more users paying you in advance. This allows you to project revenues easily.

2. You can add bolt-on subscriptions for additional features if you choose not to add them to the core.

3. Easy to administer from an accounting perspective, and they're easy for a user to understand. They know in advance what they have to pay you.

4. A full-featured free trial allows your users to get their teeth into your software and experience how good it is.

Cons

1. While subscriptions allow you to project revenue easily, they may restrict your income potential from each user. This, of course, depends on the software you've built and your users' expectations, but you may not be seeing the full revenue potential of your users.

2. You may restrict your user base, reducing your ability to monetize other areas of your technology (i.e., data)

Freemium Model

The idea behind the Freemium model is you offer a premium software solution for free with the opportunity to upgrade for even more features, or it's free for life for a majority of your user base. A classic example of Freemium is Facebook or Google. These two behemoths provide their software completely free of charge to 99% of users. They make their revenue in the data they collect from those free users (I discuss this more in the Data Monetisation Model). They then monetize that data to businesses wanting to market their products or services (Google Adwords, Facebook Ads). Pretty intelligent model, but it does need deep pockets as you need the data and LOTS of it to be able to monetize in this way.

Another example of Freemium would be Atlassian's Jira and Confluence. Why they are Freemium is because they offer almost a full version of this software completely free for life for up to 10 users. You only need to upgrade if you need advanced security features or have more users. Freemium is a great way to build your user base quickly as you reduce the barrier to entry of the need to exchange money for an unproven service. If you're building a mobile app, and are not a well-known brand already, then Freemium is the model for you as your competition on the app store is high. However, with this said, you may monetize your app in other ways, either through in-app advertising, in-app purchases, or payment in exchange for goods and services (Uber, Airbnb, etc.). These are all still considered Freemium apps. They just have different monetization strategies.

Ultimately, if you offer a superior application entirely free for life and monetize it in some other way, you're utilizing the Freemium Model in combination with one or more other models.

Pros

1. An excellent way to get mass user adoption

2. Reduced barrier to entry by not requesting cash upfront

3. A very popular, well-liked model by consumers

4. A large number of the most successful apps in the world use this model to gain mass user adoption

Cons

1. Must be combined with another Model to monetize your app/software

2. Monetisation through some model will require deep pockets to be able to keep gaining users while not receiving any revenue

In-App Advertising model

In-App Advertising is a fairly popular model in mobile apps and to a lesser extent on web apps, but essentially you get paid by advertisers for showing ads to your software users. If they click on the ad, you get paid for it. Many free apps on the app stores monetize this way, and it can be somewhat lucrative, but it does have its drawbacks. Namely in user experience.

Most users hate ads in their software and would rather you didn't advertise, but part of the benefit of upgrading is removing the ads. Of course, it does entirely depend on your app and your customer segment, as some will have no problem with ads, and others will delete your app at the sight of them. Take Facebook, for example. They put ads in your daily feed but only display those that are actually relevant to you. This means they're less annoying than a game with ads spewed all around the edges of the screen. Both, of course, are lucrative but for different reasons, and both attract different users.

. . .

I'm not suggesting you don't use in-app advertising. Just be selective with who and what you advertise and make sure these ads have little to no impact on the user experience. After all, in-app advertising can still make you seven figures plus a year in revenue. A popular way to use in-app advertising is to reward the user for watching the ad with an in-app reward. It works very well in games as the user benefits from watching a 30-60 second ad.

Pros

1. Very simple to set up

2. Generally used in combination with Freemium

3. Can be a very high revenue stream

Cons

1. If not suited to your app or customer segment, you will lose more users than you can gain

2. Can be very annoying if not appropriately positioned or deliberately positioned to force a user to click on the ad (remember the full-screen ads that pop up with a tiny little dismiss icon in the corner that all but guaranteed you'd click on the ad)

3. Unpredictable revenue income

In-App Purchases Model

Welcome to one of the holy grails of revenue models for mobile apps and game producers. In-app purchasers account for billions of dollars in revenue for software producers globally. It is by far one of the biggest revenue makers out there.

You would no doubt be familiar with in-app purchases as you most likely would have completed a purchase or two yourself, but for the sake of completeness, I'll briefly describe what it is.

An in-app purchase is a purchase a user makes from within your app in return for something that is either consumable or non-consumable. Consumables are items that can be purchased and used only once, for example, an additional life in the game, virtual money, accessories, etc. Once depleted, they cannot be used again. Non-consumables are premium features or upgrades that don't expire and can be used multiple times. An example might be a filter on a photo app or upgrading from the free to the paid version with a one-time payment (not an ongoing subscription payment).

In-app purchases are the primary source of revenue for game producers. Some still charge a fee to purchase the game, but in-app purchases for consumable upgrades and virtual in-game money is where they make a majority of their revenue. The key thing with in-app purchases is you can not make them mandatory or a necessity to use the software. Firstly users will generally pick this up fairly quickly and become annoyed, and the app stores will ban your app as it goes against their policies.

Pros

1. Very profitable and is based on your app mechanics

2. Generally used in combination with Freemium

3. Users accept and love in-app purchases if used properly

Cons

1. If not suited to your app or customer segment, you will lose more users than you can gain

2. If users are forced to use in-app purchases to use your software, you will get banned by the app stores

3. Unpredictable revenue income

Data Monetization Model

Most new startups or entrepreneurs generally overlook data monetization. However, it is one of the most lucrative monetization strategies and can be combined with all of the other models discussed above.

The fact is you will collect a lot of data about your users. Some of this data will be specific to how they use your app so you can better enhance their experience, but the rest will be data that you will very likely be able to monetize. Imagine an online web app that allows people to complete contactless menu ordering while at a venue. The venue pays for the use of the app, but the consumer just uses it to order and pay for their food and drink. Imagine you have this app in many establishments around the country, and each consumer has a personal profile. You will know what type of food they eat, what types of soft drink or beer or wine they drink, and what time of day they tend to eat and drink. That data is insanely invaluable to food and drink manufacturers. So much so they would pay you a sizeable amount to gain that level of insight as it means they know who to market to, when to market to them and what to market to them. Pure gold!!

This is just one example, but it is imperative to consider what you can do with your user data to provide an additional revenue stream. Of course, you need to make sure you have their permission to use their data and their consent, but those who opt-in are helping your software be more successful by sharing their data which you can then monetize. Even then, you can still aggregate and de-sensitize (remove the user identity from the data so they can't be identified from it) and sell this data. You still need to tell users in your privacy policy that you will use non-personally identifiable information you collect and provide it to third parties, but this is a great way to monetize data without needing explicit consent from users. In most countries, as long as the data can not be linked back to a specific user, you can use it how you want. As soon as it includes their personal information or that you will be using their data to market to them, you need their permission. Not only is this law in most countries it's just the right thing to do.

Pros

1. Can be an additional or even primary revenue stream

2. Generally used in combination with Freemium

3. Can be a very high revenue stream

4. You can generally monetize the data in more than one way

Cons

1. Generally not your first revenue stream unless you can afford to amass users without revenue

2. Unpredictable revenue income

3. Can be expensive to utilize if you haven't considered it early in your software build

4. Will require additional resources with skills in big data

Block #11 Cost Structure

Phew!! What a journey we've been on thus far. We've understood with absolute clarity who our customer is, we know who our early adopter will be, we know our customer segments problem and how our software is their Solution, we understand who our competitors are and have done a primary competitor analysis, we know what our unfair advantage is and our unique value proposition, we know how we will reach our customer segments/s, we also know our key success factors and the resources and partners we need to be successful. Finally, we know how to monetize our app.

Lastly, we need to consider ALL of the costs associated with building, maintaining, serving, supporting, and marketing our software. The Cost Structure block is there to make sure you understand what all of your costs will be. You don't need accurate numbers right now. You just need to identify where your costs will be. In this block, you need to list anything and everything that will be a cost associated with your product. The following is a list of typical expenses but is by no means exhaustive. Your industry may have regulatory fees or other licensing costs you need to consider as well.

- Marketing costs
- Sales costs
- Customer service costs
- Development costs
- Infrastructure costs
- Legal costs
- Accounting costs
- Payment gateway fees
- Appstore fees
- Staffing costs
- Government Taxes
- Supporting Software Costs (any software your staff needs to support the product and the customer, including CRM, Development IDE's, Monitoring software, Accounting software, customer service software, etc.)
- Bank fees
- Trademark and IP fees
- Business Registration fees

. . .

Congratulations!!! You've now completed the Product Model Canvas and have a greater understanding of your product than most businesses ever do. You should genuinely pat yourself on the back as this is no easy process, but if you've gotten this far, you've nailed it, and you should be proud of your accomplishment. But we're not done yet. We now have exceptional clarity ourselves, but we must directly translate that clarity into something our software developers can understand.

2

APP FEATURE & FUNCTIONALITY

In the previous chapter, we dedicated our time to gaining clarity as a Product Owner/Client, where you discovered how to utilize the Product Model Canvas to understand the 11 key pillars of your product. We're now going to shift focus to the features and functionality of your application and clearly define each one. This is where we start to translate your idea into a language developers understand while helping you to begin to visualize your application's functionality further.

When completing the following steps, it's essential to keep in mind that this isn't a technical process but a functional one. The technology underpinning your application or how your application will work has no relevance to this exercise. In most greenfield cases (developer speak for a brand new application), the technology stack that your application utilizes depends entirely on what your application needs to provide and the performance and functionality intended to the User. Even with existing applications and existing technology stacks, you should not feel constrained in any way. You may conclude your current technologies don't support your application's future vision, which means you may need to consider refactoring or rebuilding the app to ensure it will achieve your ultimate vision. If this is the case, the earlier you discover you need to refactor, the better.

We want to go into this with a sky is the limit approach because we need to provide ourselves and the developers with the complete picture. Most development agencies ignore this critical point. In nearly all cases, a client has a budget, so if they complete any in-depth discovery (most don't), they will cap everything within that constraint and only want to know about what you need to have built today. They don't consider the importance of the direction of the software, only that they are quoting on (or have been asked to create) the foundation, and that's it. And yet, the foundation of any software is critical to its long-term success, just like the foundation of a skyscraper is crucial to the long-term integrity of the building.

Further to this, most development agencies are platform or language-specific rather than being platform and language agnostic. This means they will always build your solution in the way that best suits them, which isn't necessarily what's best for you or your software. The negative outcome here is your applications' foundation may not support your future goals, which means, at worst, it needs to be rebuilt from the ground up or, at best, refactored. Either way, this can cost you all of the investment you just put into it. By capturing everything you would dream of the app doing in the future, we can make sure our initial foundation will support these future features. It also allows you to switch features out during agile development if customers want one feature over another. Furthermore, you now have a backlog and Product Roadmap documenting the future vision of the application, which both customers and investors would be keen to see.

Software Structure

Before we define the features and functionality of our application, we first need to give ourselves an idea of the software structure and the user types. We're not looking for software designs or complex diagrams that look like a solutions architect's version of a Picasso. We just need to give ourselves a basic structure to use as our basis for the next step. This exercise is all about giving us something to focus on and assisting us in gaining further clarity.

To keep this as simple as possible, most software will have two distinct components; the consumer area where your customers interact with your application and the admin area to administer your users/customers. Within these components, there will be one or more distinct user types. In most cases, we can keep this very simple and have two software components (consumer dashboard/area and admin dashboard/area) and two user types (consumer and admin). You will find this to be the most simplistic structure you can have and is the foundation of all software for you to build from. If you're unsure how many user types or components you will have, I suggest starting here and adding more as you go if your app warrants it.

. . .

The first step we need to take is to define the users of our application. A user can be considered anyone that interacts with your application in some way. You, for example, will be a user of your application and, in 99% of cases, will be the administrator. You may also have staff that will need to administer the application on your behalf but don't need the same permissions. If this is the case, I like to break this out by Super Admin (you) and Admin (your staff/ other administrators). Try to keep this as straightforward as possible while capturing the needs of your Admin functionality. The part of the application you will utilize will be the admin area or the admin dashboard. Take an A4 piece of paper, write Admin Area or Admin Dashboard, and stick it on the wall. Congratulations, you've just defined the first User/s and the first functional component of your application.

Next, we need to consider the consumer/customer and the component/s that they will utilize. In most cases, this might be the consumer dashboard or the consumer app. In other cases, you may have different types of customers with different needs or require access to an entirely different part of the software. An example might be if we were building an app for an insurance company. In this case, we would have three distinct primary user types and three distinct areas of your application. There would be the Admin Dashboard (for the Admin to administer all users of the application), the Consumer Dashboard (where consumers access all their insurance info and gain quotes and pay premiums, etc.). Finally, we have the Broker Dashboard (where the brokers can log in and prepare quotations and manage their assigned consumers). In this case, we have three distinct user types and three distinct areas of the application. As we did for the Admin Dashboard, take an A4 sheet of paper and write the consumer component/s down and stick it on the wall beside the Admin Dashboard.

Another example will be if you have a web application supported by a mobile application. In this case, you have two fronted components being Web Dashboard and Mobile App. Now that we have defined our users and the functional components of our app, it's time to begin writing Story Cards.....

Story Card Writing

Time to begin the fun part!! Writing story cards is an Agile planning method that I insist on you completing. Story card writing is where you start to talk a developer's language while keeping it in a frame you also wholly understand. This process is the beginning of the agile development cycle, so get your honorary developer hat on and let's get moving.

First, I want you to pick one of the components of your application we came up with before and focus entirely on that for now. We need to focus on a single area to start so we're not jumping all over the place, making this process very confusing and time-consuming. I would generally advise starting with your Consumer App/Consumer Dashboard (or whatever the customer-facing part of your app is) because this is where you would have already done the most critical thinking. And after all, the customer is the most crucial part of your software. And even with me discussing this in length in the previous chapter, subconsciously, you would have already focused on what features you can offer them.

As you can see from the image below, a story card consists of 3 main parts; the 'Who' (As a), the 'What' (I want to), and the 'Why' (So that I can). The 'Who' is simply the specific User the cards feature is targeting. In our example, this would be the "Consumer" (As a Consumer). The 'What' describes the physical feature, or functionality, this User wants or needs to perform within the application. In our insurance app example, this might be "I want to view my insurance premium." While the 'Why' is the purpose or reason, the User needs or wants to perform this action "So that I can understand the value of my premium and know what I need to pay." The 'Why' is the most essential part of the entire story card. It adds context to the story and therefore relays the value of providing the feature to the User in the first place. To be clear, this isn't the business value but instead the value or benefit to the User. The value associated with the 'Why' can not be underrated. Consider this for a moment; if there is no reason the User needs or wants this feature, why would we want to spend our precious resources of time and money building it in the first place. As human beings, without a compelling why we have no reason to do anything, and this is also true for a software feature. You can download our template from https://go.opsguard.io/appiphany-template-bundle-offer for a small fee.

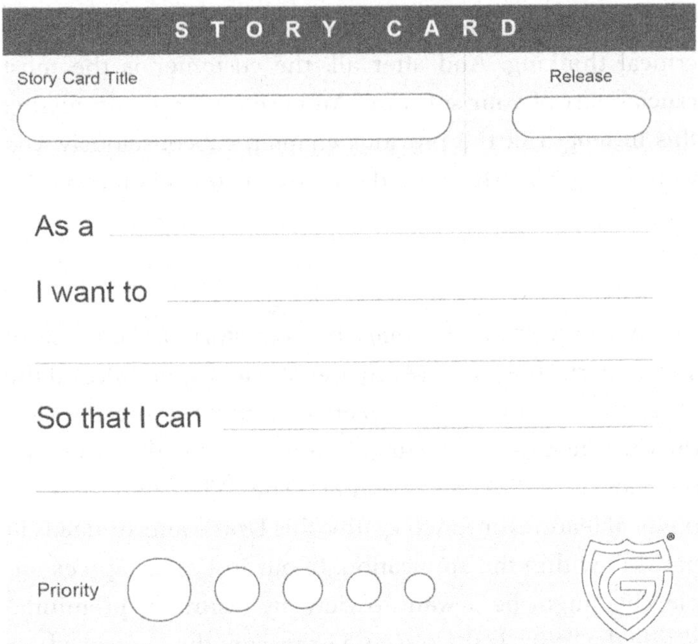
STORY CARD

Story Card Title

Release

As a

I want to

So that I can

Priority

OpsGuard™ Story Card

You'll note that our Story Card has a few extra bits to it, the 'Story Card Title' and 'Release.' The Story Card Title summarizes the story card in a few words. If we take our example story of "As a Consumer, I want to view my insurance premium so that I can understand the value of my premium and know what I need to pay," we might give this story a title of 'View My Premiums.' This title provides a nice clear and concise feature label to the card and makes it easy to know what the card describes. To simplify, it's essentially the name of your feature. As you're writing your story cards, sum them up by giving them a title. As for the 'Release' section, you can go ahead and ignore this for now, as we'll come back to that later.

You will also note that we have a 'Priority' section at the bottom of the card. Next to the 'Why,' this is a vital section, but we will also come back to that later. For now, I want you to write story cards as your life depended on them. I want you to remain focused on a single component and a single user of your application at a time until you have exhausted *ALL* of the features and functionality you can think to imagine. Remember, we want you to dream big in this exercise and pretend for the moment that we have unlimited time and budget so we can list everything we could imagine our app doing. Once you've exhausted all the features and functions you can think of for a particular user and component, you move on to the next one and repeat the process. A reminder, ***DO NOT*** complete the Priority and Release sections. We will do this once *ALL* of the features have been exhausted for all of your components and User Types.

With having done this process with 100's of clients, from startups to large corporations, I can tell you that you will struggle to think of functionality when you get to the Admin area of your app. By nature, we focus on what we can give the customer (which is fantastic) rather than what we can give ourselves. But if we cannot administer our Users, we're not going to provide them with the best customer experience. To help you with this part of the exercise, look at all of the features you just created for your Consumer Area/App and ask yourself questions like;

- What functionality or features do I need to administer the Consumers' functionality?

- How will I onboard my Consumers?

- How will I collect payment?

- How will I issue refunds?

- How can I adjust the features available to a particular Consumer if I have a multi-tiered subscription model?

- How will I report on Consumer usage?

- What user metrics of the app do I want to track?

These questions should help build a picture of how you will administer and track your Consumers' usage. If you're not considering following how your Consumers use your app, I strongly suggest you do. The better you understand how people use your software, the better the User Experience you can provide them, leading to raving fans and, therefore, more users.

The entire process, if done adequately, should take you anywhere from 4-8 hours, depending on the number of components, features, and users your app has. Once we've exhausted all of the features and functions we can think of, it's time to take a break. In our one on one Appiphany™ workshops, we always end the day and have clients sleep on this overnight. It gives you a chance to take a step back and think about the features we listed and consider anything we may have missed. Once you've taken a break, you can add anything additional you may have thought of overnight, and we're then ready for prioritization.

Prioritization

At the beginning of the Story Card writing process, you may recall that I wanted you to dream big, and the sky is the limit. Well, prioritization is where we burst that little bubble and bring ourselves back down to earth because time is limited, and so is our budget. Prioritization is all about assembling a view of what we're going to build now and what will end up in our backlog and product roadmap for future development. It will help us define our Minimum Viable Product (MVP) (i.e., our first release) and the subsequent two releases.

As you will recall, our Story Card has five circles at the bottom with the title of Priority. These five circles represent our priorities 1 through 5, with one being the largest circle and five being the smallest.

Story Card Priorities

A Priority 1 can be defined as an absolute MUST HAVE for our MVP. You need to ask yourself three questions with every story card -

- Can I get to market without this feature? and;

• Does this feature directly impact my app being able to deliver my Value Proposition? and;

• Can my software function if I don't provide this feature?

If the answer is no to all of these questions, then it is a Priority 1. Be careful with the second question relating to 'being able to deliver my Value Proposition.' There is a big difference between a feature that **delivers** your value prop, and one the **supports** it.

A Priority 2 is also a MUST HAVE but with the vital difference that it doesn't **need** to be in the MVP. A Priority 2 is what I call a fast follow feature. It's a feature that supports our Value Proposition, but we can get to market without it, and the software still functions if it's not delivered. I like to think of a Priority 2 as a feature that we'll deliver in our MVP if we have time and budget, but if we run out of these resources, it can be in our next release.

A Priority 3 can be defined as a SHOULD HAVE. It's a feature that will add significant value to our application and supports our overall Value Proposition. But, we know we can wait to deliver this feature within the next 3-6months after launch. Our Priority 3's are our follow-up value add features that keep our users hooked on our app. They're features that we know we can wait to deliver but will retain and increase user engagement.

A Priority 4 feature can be defined as a COULD HAVE. While it adds value, it is either too large for us to deliver in our current budgets or is a little bit on the dreamland side of our existing resources. We're utterly comfortable if we cannot provide this feature in the next 6-12 months, but we know it supports our value proposition. These features generally sit in the 12-month+ time frame on our roadmap and may not be delivered at all.

And lastly, our Priority 5 can be defined as a future feature that we know can wait and are the long-term goals or aspirations of the application. These are the features that if they never get delivered for two or more years, we're still exceeding our customers' expectations and leaving our competitors behind.

To begin the prioritization process, I want you to take a marker pen of a particular color (blue, green, red, pink, it doesn't matter), and just like we did with writing story cards, we're going to focus on one component at a time. I want you to read through each story card and ask yourself the three Priority 1 questions;

- Can I get to market without this feature? and;
- Does this feature directly impact my app being able to deliver my Value Proposition? and;
- Can my software function if I don't provide this feature?

Following the Priority guide in the paragraphs above, I want you to color in the circle of the selected Priority for each feature with your chosen marker pen. Continue this process for all of the features in each component previously defined, remembering to stay focused on that single component at a time. Once you complete one component, move on to the next until all of the features have a priority allocated. Congratulations, you've just completed the first round of prioritization!!

Now that you've completed the first round, I want you to rearrange all of your Story Cards into their Priority groups while still keeping them within their components. This means I want you to group all of your Priority 1's, 2's, 3's, etc. together with your one's being at the top and the five's at the bottom without mixing up your components (it's ok if the different user types under the same component are mixed here if any). Leave a little space between each priority group so we're able to shuffle things around. Lastly, draw a line under your Priority ones, separating them from the rest.

After all that shuffling, take a step back and look at the masterpiece that is your application. You now have your first accurate glimpse at the scale and size of your application and your first chance to start to visualize what it might take to build it. I want you to look at the size of your Priority ones. Remember this is your MVP and the first thing you're delivering to the market. In most cases, this is also what you're asking your developers to provide a quotation for, so it directly impacts your current budget. I will almost guarantee your wall will have more Priority ones than any other Priority, and that's ok at this stage. In the 100's of these I've done, I can say about 3% of people will nail their Priorities on the first cut. Because by nature, we will see everything as a Priority one. However, by grouping them into their priority groups and taking a step back, we begin to visualize the scale of what we're expecting to deliver in our MVP release. Visualizing the scale helps us ground ourselves and provides insight that just maybe some of those features can wait until the next release.

In our second prioritization pass, we will repeat the process as before, but we're only focussing on our Priority 1's, 2's, and 3's. We're going to ask ourselves the same questions of our Priority 1's as before, but we need to be brutal here with our answers. I want you to use a different color marker pen for this exercise than before, so it's easy to identify a feature we reprioritized.

Starting with your Priority ones, ask yourself;

• Can I **REALLY** get to market without this feature? and;

• Does this feature **REALLY** impact my app being able to deliver my Value Proposition? and;

• Will my software **REALLY** not function if I don't provide this feature?

I want you to challenge yourself with these questions and, as previously mentioned, be brutal. For anything you decide to reprioritize, take your different color marker and put a line through the old circle and color in your new chosen Priority. In most cases, this will simply be changing a Priority 1 to a Priority 2. Repeat this exercise for your Priority 2's and 3's.

. . .

It's important to note that you're not just looking to reprioritize down, but you can also move a priority up. For example, you may be able to argue that a Priority 2 really should be a 1, and that's ok just don't get carried away swapping out the features you just moved down. In most cases, we see Priority 3's becoming 2's rather than 2's becoming 1's. Once you've gone through this process, rearrange your cards as before, and bask in the glory that is your application. Remember, a Priority 2 is something that we will get into our MVP if we have time and budget; otherwise, it will follow quickly after that. An easy way to think of it is that a Priority 2 will answer 2 out of the three questions. In contrast, a Priority 1 answers all three questions while a Priority 3 answers only one question.

We're now ready to move on to the next phase, documenting everything we've just done. This document will not only be a sensational asset for you but will be the document you will ask your developers to utilize to provide an estimate. When we do this for clients, we call this the build bible.

3

DOCUMENT YOUR IDEA

Time for the rubber to hit the road. This chapter is the part where you take all of the tremendous work you've completed thus far and get it all down into a well-structured, crystal clear document. This is the document you're going to use to ask your in-house developers or external development agency to estimate against. They're going to use this document as their guiding star. It will become their build bible while being a primary reference document with all of the features and functionality the developers need to build.

When we produce these documents for our one on one Appiphany™ clients, they generally take us 2-3 days to write. This is because we also design your infrastructure and recommend language and technology stacks. Additionally, we create a whole bunch of flow diagrams for user models and onboarding, etc. Of course, I don't expect the document you produce at the end of this chapter is that extensive as it does take a lot of technical experience to provide that much detail. But what I do expect is that you can now document your product and the feature requirements in great detail.

To begin with, I want you to take all of your story cards and transfer them to an excel workbook. You can download our template from https://go.opsguard.io/appiphany-template-bundle-offer for a small fee. You can also create a basic version of your own with the following headings; Title, Story, Priority, and Release. Once complete this spreadsheet with all of your stories, you will have just created your Product Backlog.

As part of the Appiphany™ Template Bundle, you can also download a basic word template you can use as a starting point for your document and is the basis for the Appiphany™ Build Bible we complete. If you prefer to create your own, it should have the following structure; Cover Page, Contents, Executive Summary, Structure & Users, Software Features, and Product Backlog.

To begin with, take all the data you produced in your Product Model canvas and sum up your idea. You don't need to detail every block of the Product Model Canvas. You just need to take all that knowledge and sum it up in a few paragraphs (4-5 is usually enough). This summary forms the basis of your software's introduction to your developers, giving them a snapshot of what you want to be built, who you're targeting, and why you're going to kick your competitors' butt (Executive Summary). Give as much detail as you can, as this is the foundation that your developers will pin all of your features to and help those features make sense.

Next, we will list our software components and the Users we have defined in our agile discovery session (Structure & Users). We then write out all of our software features, starting with Priority 1 and moving through to Priority 3. You're also very welcome to include your Priority 4's and 5's but make it clear to your developer you do not want these estimated (Software Features). As a general rule, we leave these out of the Appiphany™ Build Bible because even when instructed not to quote them, many agencies go ahead and add them in any way, which confuses the quotes you get back. Instead, you can create two versions, one for yourself with all your features listed and one for your developers to quote with only those in Priority 1 through 3. From a quotation perspective, the purpose of this document is to allow you to compare apples with apples when different agencies provide you with their estimates.

When completing your Software Features section, be sure to group the features under the Component and then group them by their priority. For example, if you have a component called 'Consumer App,' you would create a heading called Consumer App and then add a sub-title of Priority One. You would list out all of your Priority one features and create another sub-heading for Priority 2 and so on. If you have more than one User Type under your components, you don't need to group them under a separate heading. However, grouping your features under their respective Component makes it easier for your developer to understand what they're looking at. Also, grouping them under your Priorities makes it easy to see what's essential for that Component and what might be able to wait.

Under the Software Features Heading, create a sub-heading for each Component (as per the example above). Under the component heading, start a sub-heading for your Priorities 1 through 3 (remember we only want an estimate on these as they are the ones that matter the most to us now). Starting with the Consumer Component, begin writing out all the Titles you gave your story cards within that Component under its appropriate priority. The title will be the paragraph heading for that feature. I want you to now describe that feature in as much detail as possible. You're essentially taking the straightforward story card and writing several detailed paragraphs about it. The more descriptive you are, the more clarity you're providing your developer. I want to reiterate that I don't want you to hold back here. Be as descriptive as possible but don't write sentences for the sake of writing them. Everything you write needs to be clear and concise yet descriptive enough to provide the critical thing we're looking to provide; Clarity. If we continue with our example story in Chapter 2, 'View My Premiums,' we would want to describe as much information as possible. Including how we create premiums (are they sourced from a database, or do we have a separate engine/app that calculates them, or does our app need to create them on the fly), how are they displayed (monthly/yearly, etc.), is there an expiry, and are they live or fixed. Continuing with this example, if another app/engine calculates the premiums, how do we communicate with this (i.e., is there an API (Application Programming Interface) or other means of communicating with it). If in a database, what kind of database and where does it live (on-premise or in the cloud). Finally, if our app needs to generate these calculations on the fly, where do we source the data from, and what is the math we need to use?

As you can see, that one story card can contain a lot of information, and you must provide as much detail as you have the knowledge to offer.

More explicit and concise details = absolute developer clarity.

As a developer, we would break this card down into smaller stories but don't worry about that for now, as your job is to detail the feature. The developers' job will be to break it down further into smaller pieces of work if needed. Just describe your features in as much detail as possible.

You're doing awesome!! This task can be daunting, but it's super critical to get it right. Feel free to go over this several times before you feel you've completed it. Once you've listed the features for all components within their priorities (1 through 3), you're ready to insert your Backlog. Take the excel sheet you created earlier and insert it into the document under your Product Backlog heading.

A massive **congratulations** are in order as you've just completed your very own mini Build Bible!!! You can now take this document and have your developers or an external agency quote from it. I promise you will blow away 99% of agencies you take this to. Most of them never create something for clients to this level of detail, let alone receive something like this to quote.

Now let's learn the secrets development agencies don't want you to know and learn how to select your developer.

4

SELECTING YOUR DEVELOPER

The effort you have put in so far has been nothing short of stellar! But we're not done yet. Unfortunately, this part can be one of the most daunting and, sadly, the most costly in the entire process. Development agencies come in all shapes and sizes, and they all have different ways of working, quoting, and supporting (if at all) your software once they've completed the build. But what you may not realize is you have many options as to how your software is built and by whom. This chapter aims to give you the inside knowledge to help you navigate the minefield that is outsourced development and show you there are other options.

As an industry veteran who has owned several agencies over the years, not only have I learned how to give clients what they want, but also the shady and sometimes appalling habits of others. At OpsGuard™, we don't expect our clients to complete their development with us after completing their Appiphany™ workshop, but most do.

However, we always encourage them to obtain quotes from other agencies using their Appiphany™ Build Bible because we want them to know with confidence if they choose us, they're working with the best. But further to this, we want them to understand the value of the build bible we just produced. As mentioned in the last chapter, even if you've followed the instructions and created your own less detailed version, 99% of agencies will be blown away by this level of detail. Typically agencies get a one or two-pager and are asked to quote from it. Such a simple document makes it very difficult for you to compare apples with apples. One developer will interpret it one way, while another will look at it entirely differently. With the detailed structure and clarity provided by the build bible, the only differentiator will be the technology stack and development language the agency recommends (and, of course, their price point in the market).

I've broken this chapter into several sections to take you through different topics, including your developer options, what to look out for, the right questions to ask, and how to protect your IP. I'm also going to outline what you should demand from your developer, and if they are reluctant or refuse to do any of these things, I strongly suggest you run in the other direction. All you're asking for is transparency, communication, and quality which really shouldn't be too much to ask. Let's dive in with the first section.

Developer Options

I want to make sure you understand you have several options for developing your software, and working with an agency is only one of those options. I've outlined each below and given you some pros and cons.

1. **Development agencies** - An agency are an established team (or teams) of developers that constantly move from project to project and build software based on what a client wants. They are normally language and technology stack specific and can be what we call onshore (within your country), offshore (generally South East Asia, South America or Eastern Europe) and hybrid (a combination of onshore and offshore) teams. They typically bill you on an hourly, weekly, or sometimes fixed cost basis (this is very rare). They also usually consist of a mixture of senior and junior developers and will sometimes employ other skilled people such as UI/UX experts, Marketing experts, Quality Assurance (QA), and Testing experts.

Pros

• Generally well-established teams with a mix of Senior and Junior developers

• Can provide a broad team of experts with skillsets across all areas of development and sometimes even marketing (a one-stop-shop)

• The good ones come with references

• Generally a safe way to get started

• An excellent option to build your Minimum Viable Product and first few releases

• Some are even set up to support you long term and be your permanent development team

• Some will fully integrate you into the development process and provide complete transparency

Cons

• The danger of working with an entirely offshore team and not being made aware of it

• If not adequately managed, costs can overrun

• Very few will do detailed scoping, which means their estimates are flawed

• There's no one to validate and check the code they produce is of appropriate quality (you don't know what you're getting unless you understand code yourself or have a third party that can check it)

• Very few will complete or maintain adequate documentation for your software

• You will generally have little control over their way of working and day to day tasks

• The risk of little to no handover to any new developers

• Once your project ends or one of their developers leaves, you run the risk of losing retained knowledge of your application and how it works

• Some agencies will split developers time across multiple projects at once, which means your project doesn't get the respect it deserves

. . .

2. Employing Full-Time Developers - Full-time developers are your employees that you have to pay a regular salary, pay taxes for, and 401k or superannuation. They also have leave and sick pay entitlements, along with any other statutory or additional benefits you want to offer. You will typically start with one or two senior developers, and they will normally be skilled in the language and technology stack specific to your software. They are long-term hires and require you have the revenue/capital to pay them. They also require management and oversight. They will rarely have any knowledge or skills in UI/UX and Marketing but should have knowledge and skills in QA and Testing.

Pros

- You have complete control and oversight in what they do
- You will usually guarantee retention of knowledge
- You can control the quality of documentation
- You know they're only working on your project
- They're your developers and will typically have more passion about the project than an agency might
- If you employ experienced seniors, you can generally be assured the quality of what they produce is acceptable

Cons

- They won't commonly have a broad skill set in all the areas you need (design, UI/UX, Branding, Marketing, etc.) which means employing more people

- They're full-time employees, which means you have all the costs associated with that, including salary, taxes, benefits, retirement funds, and any other statutory costs (insurances, etc.)
- You need to have the capital to pay them for 12 months
- You need to manage them or employ a manager
- You will typically need to buy them the equipment and software they need to develop your software (desktops, monitors, development software)

3. **Employing Contract Developers** - Contract developers are typically sourced from an external recruitment agency and are compensated at a daily rate. You will have the ability to contract as many or as few contractors that will work for your project and naturally require some kind of leadership/management. They can be skilled in any area you need and are available for both very short and long periods of engagement.

Pros

- Very flexible
- You can build a team of varying skillsets
- Easily scalable
- Normally available very quickly
- You control the level of transparency

• They're essentially your staff for the time you contract them

• They will be dedicated to your project

Cons

• Very expensive and usually are 2-3 times more expensive than the full-time equivalent

• They need oversight and constant management

• Their code quality very's and may still require technical oversight

• You will need to abide by the recruitment agencies terms of service

• Normally a fixed term and minimum of 6-month contract (some do offer hourly rates with no fixed term and even month to month)

4. Employing a Project Manager or Interim/Full-time CTO to manage all of the above - A fourth additional option is to employ a Project Manager or Interim/Full-time Chief Technology Officer to oversee any/all of the above options. This person has extensive technology, product, and project experience that provides oversight over the project and developers and ensures your project stays on track. They can be either full-time, part-time employees or contractors and should be knowledgeable in all areas of development, including UI/UX, QA, and Testing. They will likely not be skilled in Marketing. Their compensation is the same as a full-time employee or contractor above.

. . .

Pros

- Manages and provides complete oversight on your behalf
- Will provide a no rubbish assessment of your project and developers
- With the right skills can ensure the quality of the code and documentation is of an adequate standard

A CTO can also develop your long term technology strategy

Cons

- An additional cost on top of the above options
- They will typically only ever be available part-time
- Their time will be split between more than one project
- While knowledgeable in all areas, they will not likely be experts

Selection Process

Now that you understand the different options you have available. I want to give you guidance over the selection process of each of these and the sorts of questions you should be asking, along with a few non-negotiable items.

Development Agencies

The first thing I want to highlight is that not all agencies are created equal. You will need to ask the right questions to get to right answers. Agencies are a great option, but there are a few things to consider before deciding if an agency is one you can be confident employing. From creating your build bible above, the only real variable you need to contend with is what technology stack the agency will suggest or want to build your software in (unless you have professional advice or technical knowledge and have already made this decision).

As previously mentioned, most agencies will specialize in one to two programming languages and infrastructure stacks, so they will always recommend building what they know best. You might be thinking, "Oh well, I only want to build a mobile app on iPhone, so I only need to worry about that." And for the most part, you would be right. However, you also have the option of cross-development platforms such as React Native, PhoneGap, Xamerin, and Flutter. These options allow you to build both iOS and Android applications simultaneously. And for a large number of applications, they're more than sufficient. For example, Instagram, Bloomberg, Pinterest, Skype, and Telsa all use React Native to build their mobile applications. However, some mobile apps need access to platform-specific libraries or are highly customized on each platform and therefore need to be developed in the native Swift (iOS) or Java (Android) languages. The point being, developing your application in the native language is not always the only nor best option, especially from a financial perspective.

The other alternative and what is becoming more popular these days are mobile responsive web applications. These are applications that run on their own servers and are accessed through the users' web browser on their mobile and desktop devices. The term mobile responsive means the same application can be accessed on a users' mobile, tablet, and desktop device. They will have relatively similar User Interfaces for each while being served to the user via a browser. You are limited to some degree by what you can do on a mobile or tablet device with a web application. But if your software doesn't need access to any device-specific libraries, or doesn't warrant building a mobile app, then a web application is a great choice. It also has the benefit of not needing to download another app onto a users' phone. Many Software as a Service (SaaS) based applications are web applications, and some build free mobile apps to support their web-based counterparts. Examples would be the Atlassian suite of applications, Hubspot, Salesforce, Shopify, most Banks, Xero, Quickbooks, etc. In all of these cases, the mobile application is a simplified version of the web application with only the features that make sense to be on mobile. Some of the languages you can build web applications with are; Ruby on Rails, ReactJS, Angular, Node JS, PHP, Python, and many more.

I've no doubt confused you a little here, and that's ok. I don't expect you to understand all of what I've mentioned above completely. The main point I want you to take away is that you have options. Just because an agency prefers or has the skills to develop your application in a particular language or tech stack doesn't mean that tech stack is the best option for **your** app. I highly recommend you work with a language-agnostic agency as you're then working with someone that will build the application in the technology that is best suited to what you want it to do today and where you see it in the future.

"Just because an agency prefers or has the skills to develop your application in a particular language or tech stack doesn't mean that tech stack is the best option for your app."

The next thing I want you to consider is where your agency is located. As discussed above, you have three types of agencies; onshore (within your countries borders), offshore (outside your countries borders), and a hybrid of the two with both onshore and offshore teams.

Offshore Agencies

Offshore agencies can be fraught with danger. Unless you know what you're doing or have an experienced Interim/Full-time CTO, or they're a reputable agency in a respected country, I strongly suggest steering well clear of them. The number of horror stories I've heard over the years is countless, and unfortunately, things don't seem to be getting much better. While working with a purely overseas agency can be cheaper than working with one onshore, I have found their care factor is even less than some onshore agencies. Essentially, a large number of them are what we call in the industry code chop shops. They just want to churn and burn as much code as possible, reusing whatever they can to pump the software out and move on to the next project. You are very limited with IP and confidentiality protection in most cases, and the code's quality is sometimes shocking. There are even cases where we've been asked to fix or review software that these agencies have developed only to sit bewildered about how it even functions at all. Over the years, I have seen tens of millions of dollars wasted as clients end up needing to rebuild the solution from scratch.

Now I'm not saying all offshore agencies are harmful. There are certainly exceptions to this rule, but unless you know what you're doing, I suggest steering clear of those in the following emerging regions; South East Asia, South America, Africa, parts of the Middle East, and Eastern Europe. To reiterate, there are some exceptionally talented developers in the regions I've just mentioned, but unless you have development and project management experience, engage them at your own risk. The moral of the story is to stick to reputable agencies in respectable countries. An example is working with an Australian or Canadian agency if you're in the US or UK. Due to the exchange rate, you're generally going to get the development cheaper, and you won't have issues with language barriers. Regardless of whom you choose to work with or location, make sure they're a ***reputable*** agency and ask for a reference or two that you can physically speak with, not just one that's written.

Onshore Agencies

Onshore agencies are without a doubt a safer option, but you still need to be careful and make sure they're not fly by nighters or there to take your money and run. Usually, you can avoid these agencies by speaking with a couple of references and a quick google search. You also want to make sure your onshore agency isn't just a front for an offshore operation. This doesn't mean it's not ok for them to have developers offshore. OpsGuard™, for example, has developers in 20 countries around the globe, but we've built that from humble beginnings and have registered companies and offices in 3 of those countries. I'm referring to the one-person offices with LLCs in the US (or Pty Ltd in Australia), and their entire dev team and operation is located overseas. Again, this may not be bad, but if they're not upfront about it, you have no idea where your data is stored, which can lead to privacy issues. Furthermore, you might be wanting to ask why they weren't upfront about it in the first place.

The safety net you have with onshore and hybrid agencies with a legal entity in your country is primarily around confidentiality and IP. If they have a legal presence in your country, then you have a much better chance of successful litigation in the most extreme of circumstances. The other positive of onshore agencies is you will be able to pick up the phone and talk to someone during standard business hours.

Further in this chapter, I give you a list of requirements you should demand from your development agency regardless of their location. One of these is a particular way of working with them (a daily standup) which becomes much easier if you're in the same, or at least a similar time zone where there is a reasonable amount of crossover.

Hybrid Agencies

Hybrid agencies are simply a blend of onshore and offshore. OpsGuard is an excellent example of a hybrid agency as we have offices in 3 countries and staff in 20 at the time of writing this book. These agencies provide clients with the potential for 24-hour development and support, delivering apps even faster. When one team finishes for the day, the next team can pick up where they left off.

All the same warnings still apply though. As previously discussed, many one-person local companies act as a front for offshore agencies. The next thing to consider is where your data is stored. For some, there is no issue with data being held overseas, but there are several cases where you may not want that to be the case. I suggest asking the hybrid agency where they intend on storing your data or request it's stored in your region.

So now that we understand the different types of agencies and what to look out for, let's dive into the actual selection process and the questions you should be asking.

Agency Selection Criteria & Questions

Selecting an agency to work with is a relatively simple process. Below I've given you a list of absolute must-haves from a selection perspective and a list of questions you should ask every agency you consider hiring. The criteria's sole purpose is about protecting you and ensuring you'll get the best outcome possible.

Criteria

I strongly recommend you only work with agencies that meet or are willing to meet the following criteria;

• Can provide references you can speak with (emails are ok but make sure it's a registered domain and not just a Gmail address. Otherwise, it's difficult to be confident the person you're speaking with is legitimate)

• Are a full-service agency that can deliver everything from ideation through to post-go-live support (some even provide marketing, but at the very least, they must be able to build, support, and maintain your software **and** infrastructure)

• Are willing to provide or sign a written contract that has solid confidentiality and IP protection

• Have a physical and legal entity in your country

• Are programming language and technology stack agnostic (this will be tough to find, but they do exist, and it's in your best interest to not just go with any old language or stack)

• Provide you with a dedicated client manager

• Are willing to commit to daily standups with you present and involved (I explain this further in Chapter 7, but in short, a standup is a quick 10-15min daily meeting **with** the development team working on your app)

• Offer some kind of warranty period post go live (this is about fixing bugs that come up after you launch and not about adding new features or tweaking UI)

• Offer a solid support plan post go live (this is post-warranty support & maintenance)

- Have experience in the language your app is built on and infrastructure your app is to be hosted on
- Are willing to provide detailed developer documentation (this is critical if you ever want to move to a different agency or employ your own developers one day as it dramatically reduces the learning curve and gets them up to speed on your app faster)
- Are willing to write and provide automated test scripts as part of their build
- Have a dedicated QA/Test team/engineer on your project (this is about ensuring the quality of your codebase and that proper testing has occurred before handing it over to you or your customers)
- Are willing to ensure the git repository used to store and version manage your code is **YOURS**, and you have complete access and control over it (this is your code and **your IP**, so you want to be in control of it and you want your developers to use only your git repository and not fork it (copy it) anywhere else. Most agencies will be happy with this and might even set it up for you)
- Are willing to take the time and walk through your build bible with you while your developer/s are present before they begin cutting code (usually this is in the form of an onboarding meeting and your entire dev team from UI/UX through to testers are present)

If your agency is willing to or already provides all of the above, you can rest assured you're in safe hands and your risks are dramatically reduced.

Questions

The following questions are primarily based on the criteria above, but I've included them as a checklist for you. You can also download this checklist for free https://go.opsguard.io/hubfs/Appiphany/Development-Agency-Selection-Criteria-and-Questions.pdf;

- Can you provide references I can email or speak to of clients you have worked with before?

- What services do you provide as an agency?

- Do you offer a detailed scoping session?

- Do you offer post-development warranties, and if so, for how long?

- Do you have experience with the language you're proposing, and if so, on how many projects?

- Do you have skills in other languages or platforms that might be better suited to my application?

- What kind of contract do you offer?

- Where are your offices located and how many staff do you have?

- Where are the developers located that will be working on my project?

- Will I have someone I can speak to if I have questions or concerns?

- Can I join or have a daily 10-minute meeting with the developers working on my project?

- Will your developers, write and maintain detailed documentation with the software

- Will you produce any automated test scripts as part of your development?

- Do you have a dedicated QA or test team to maintain code quality?

- Are you willing to work from my git repository and not fork my project outside of this for any reason?

Full-time Developers

Developing software from the ground up is an exhilarating endeavor. Even today, after being involved in hundreds of software projects, I still get a buzz when the first line of code is cut. You're bringing something to life that will hopefully positively impact millions of people's lives. Full-time developers are a great option to build your software and provide a large amount of flexibility. You have complete control over the development process and methodologies used, which means you can effortlessly implement the systems and strategies mentioned in this book. Furthermore, you can easily have the team run using Agile Methodologies (explained in Chapter 7) and control the documentation process.

However, the best time to employ full-time developers is if you already have existing software and are ready to take it to the next level. While you can build your application from scratch with your own developers, you will need to have both the financial resources, management structure, and the time it will take to onboard them and build the first release.

In this case, you're normally only hiring one developer to de-risk yourself when you haven't yet validated your idea. I made the mistake in one of my early startups of employing a full-time developer straight off the bat. Don't get me wrong, he was terrific, but the time it took to build the beta release was more than double had I engaged an agency.

To clarify this further, the developers' annual salary at the time was circa $110,000 (total cost to me including taxes, benefits, etc.), and it took 8.5 months to build the MVP. It, therefore, cost $77,916.67 to deliver the software, and had I spent the same amount with an agency, I would have gotten the app to market in only 3-4 months. This scenario was back in the early 2000s when developers were much cheaper than they are today.

The correct number of developers to employ will depend on several factors, including your software, finances, and time constraints. Unless you have the financial resources, it's doubtful you're going to employ 2-3 senior developers to build your first one or two versions. The other thing you need to consider is these devs are not the only employees you'll need on the team. You'll also need a UI/UX expert to design the software in the first place and possibly testers and QA engineers (although the devs can also perform these two roles). Your full-time developers will also need to be experienced in DevOps and designing and managing cloud infrastructure efficiently. Otherwise, you'll also need to employ developers with these skill sets. Lastly, your devs will need to be skilled in all of the languages your software needs to be built-in, including backend and frontend.

. . .

I don't want to turn you off of the idea of employing developers as they are a great option. However, I want you to be aware that it's not just as simple as hiring one or two people to get the job done. You need to build a team around them to ensure you have all the skills you need.

As previously mentioned, if you don't have the financial capacity to build the team, the best time to bring on full-timers is when you have your MVP built, have an additional capital injection, and have revenue flowing in. However, there is an alternate option whereby you employ one full-time developer to oversee an agency's work. This individual is then responsible for QA and will be the primary source of knowledge when you're ready to build the team later. The only downside to this idea is they will be an additional cost on top of your agency, although they will offset this by a small amount given they will do some of the work.

The below will give you a rough break down of the costs associated with a full-time development team and what you can expect;

Senior Developer (backend/full-stack) = circa $130,000 - $200,000+

Senior Developer (mobile iOS/Android/React Native) = circa $145,000 - $200,000+

Junior Developer (either backend or mobile) = circa $80,000+

Senior UI/UX Expert = circa $125,000+

DevOps Engineer = circa $120,000+

Test Engineers = circa $85,000+

These numbers are based on employing talent in the US within these roles, and the Australian figures don't differ all that much, so this is a relatively good guide to give you a starting point.

You can offer employee shares in return for a reduced salary. Unfortunately, due to the shortage of skilled developers on the market at the time of writing, employers are offering both standard levels of compensation in addition to employee shares and employee benefits.

Full-Time Developer Selection Criteria & Questions

Like all full-time employees, you will have all of the overheads that come with this, so you need to make sure the people you choose to be a part of the team will excel in their role. After all, employees aren't a short-term commitment and will hopefully be a part of your business for years to come.

The below list is by no means extensive and will vary depending on what you're building, but it will give you a solid foundation. If you struggle with any of these points, it might be worth considering using an Interim CTO to join the interviews and set up the initial management oversight.

Criteria

- If you're building a new team, you will want Senior Developers as your foundation. To be considered Senior, a developer will have 3-5+ years of experience in the particular language and tech stack you're building your app with

- They should be proficient in more than one language

- They should understand DevOps and how to create and build deployment pipelines

- They should have a good understanding of the infrastructure you want to host your app on

- The perfect developer will have frontend, backend, and mobile skills

- They should be able to pass coding and error checking tests

Questions

The following is a list of standard interview questions. Again, if you don't understand the technology, I suggest using an Interim CTO to test the candidate's technical knowledge while you're assessing their personality and fit for your business. I like to understand the individual before I evaluate their capability. Their resume tells me they have the skills for the role, or they wouldn't have gotten an interview in the first place. Once I understand their personality and fit in the team and then test the skills and experience in their resume isn't a fabrication.

- Tell me a little about yourself? What do you like to do on the weekends?

- Tell me your favorite project to date and why?

- Describe for me a situation where you were challenged with a development task. How did you overcome this challenge? What steps did you take?

- What's the longest amount of time you've spent on a single project?

- If you're doing pair programming and have a fundamental difference of opinion with how a particular function should be written with your partner, how would you go about resolving this?

- Tell me about your agile knowledge. What methodologies have you used in the past?

- Who would your role model in the world of tech be and why?

- You've pushed a piece of code live, and it brings down the entire application. Describe in detail the steps you would take to resolve the issue.

- You've finished a sprint, and the team is completing their retrospective. Someone points out an issue with something you've done during the sprint that could be improved. How do you respond?

- What experience do you have with API's and can you describe the process for developing them?

- Do you have any projects you're working on in your spare time?

- You get a call from your team lead at 6 am saying your application has intermittent issues allowing users access. At first glance, it looks like the issue is with a load balancer managed by the DevOps team. How do you proceed?

• Describe a time you noticed a team member was struggling, and you proactively reached out to help them.

• A bug appears in your application, creating serious issues with performance and one of the key features. Describe how you would diagnose and fix the issue

• What do you think are the most critical aspects when reviewing another team member's code?

• Do you consider unit testing essential or a waste of time?

• Can you describe Object-Oriented Programming and its core components?

All of these questions will give you a solid insight into the candidates' abilities and experience and how they handle certain situations. They also provide insight if the person will just get in and get the job done or want to pass the buck on to someone else. I could list many more questions, but these are the main ones I use when interviewing our developers.

The last thing I would suggest doing is a technical assessment and mini-trial project they need to complete to prove their technical knowledge and abilities. Having an Interim/Full-time CTO comes in handy in this situation because they can assess the outcome and decide if the person has the skills needed.

Contract Developers

Contract developers are a great option if you need additional resources to support an internal or external team.

They essentially act as your full-time employees for the period you've engaged them. The most significant risk you run when developing software with contractors is knowledge attrition with how your solution or a particular part of your solution works when they leave. This is why they must document their work (just like an agency), so when the next developer picks up the code, it's easy to identify how it works and therefore reduces the time it will take for them to get up to speed.

The primary drawback of contract developers is the cost. You will spend somewhere between 1.8-2.5 times more per contractor than a full-time employee. Because in most cases, contractors sourced via a recruitment agency who will add their fee on top of the daily rate your contractor wants. The contractor also has to take into account paying their own taxes and statutory benefits. As an example, let's say a full-time developers' annual salary for a role is circa $145,000. That equates to approximately $604.16/day. The same contract developer would likely cost you somewhere between $980/day and $1,200/day. That's a huge difference, so not really recommended for your first build and certainly not over the long term.

However, contractors do have a place if you need them to support your in-house team for short periods. An agency would still likely be better and work out more cost-effective in the long run if they're willing to let you embed their developers in your team.

Criteria

- Your contractors should be Senior Developers. To be considered Senior, a developer will have 3-5+ years of experience in the particular language and tech stack you're building your app with

- They should be proficient in more than one language

- They should understand DevOps and how to create build and deployment pipelines

- They should have a good understanding of the infrastructure you want to host your app on

- The perfect developer will have frontend, backend, and mobile skills

- They should be able to pass coding and error checking tests

Questions

The same interview questions apply for a contractor as a full-time developer. Once again, If you don't understand the technology, then I suggest using an Interim CTO to test the candidate's technical knowledge while you assess their personality and fit for your business. In some cases, the contracting agency will have already evaluated this for you and will guarantee the contractor's skills.

- Tell me a little about yourself? What do you like to do on the weekends?

- Tell me your favorite project to date and why?

- Describe for me a situation where you were challenged with a development task. How did you overcome this challenge? What steps did you take?

- What's the longest amount of time you've spent on a single project?

- If you're doing pair programming and have a fundamental difference of opinion with how a particular function should be written with your partner, how would you go about resolving this?

- Tell me about your agile knowledge. What methodologies have you used in the past?

- Who would your role model in the world of tech be and why?

- You've pushed a piece of code live, and it brings down the entire application. Describe in detail the steps you would take to resolve the issue.

- You've finished a sprint, and the team is completing their retrospective. Someone points out an issue with something you've done during the sprint that could be improved. How do you respond?

- What experience do you have with API's and can you describe the process for developing them?

- Do you have any projects you're working on in your spare time?

- You get a call from your team lead at 6 am saying your application has intermittent issues allowing users access. At first glance, it looks like the issue is with a load balancer managed by the DevOps team. How do you proceed?

- Describe a time you noticed a team member was struggling, and you proactively reached out to help them.

• A bug appears in your application, creating serious issues with performance and one of the key features. Describe how you would diagnose and fix the issue

• What do you think are the most essential aspects when reviewing another team member's code?

• Do you consider unit testing essential or a waste of time?

• Can you describe Object-Oriented Programming and its core components?

As you can see, all of these questions are identical to a full-time developer. The critical thing with a contractor is you have a little more flexibility if you're not happy with them, as your contract agent will typically give you a replacement if you're not satisfied. Additionally, you may not need to test technical abilities as the contract agent should have already done this.

Interim/Full-Time CTO or Project Manager

I like to think of an Interim/Full-time CTO as an insurance policy to manage and oversee all of the above options. They can also design your software and technology vision giving you foresight the other options may not provide. Of course, they are an additional cost, but you are de-risking your entire technology division by bringing them on. Interim CTOs work the same as contractors, whereby you pay them a daily rate, and they are your 'employees' for the duration of the engagement. However, unlike contract developers, you will usually only employ them two days a week, reducing your overall financial commitment while still getting the same benefits as a full-time CTO.

Similarly, a Project Manager also de-risks your development and can provide oversight to any of the above options. The most notable difference is they're only going to be focused on project delivery and not necessarily the quality of what's being built. A good CTO, on the other hand, will have both quality and delivery as priorities. Another benefit both of these options provide is the ability to call out agencies, contractors, and full-time employees if they're not entirely upfront with you.

Criteria

The following is a set of criteria for a CTO;

• Ideally 8-10 years experience as a CTO or Senior Team Leader

• A broad and in-depth level of technical experience

• Strong leadership and management capabilities

• Ideally experienced in building apps within your market or vertical

• Exceptional technology strategy prowess

• Experience being involved in and managing multiple projects

• Exceptional understanding of the entire product lifecycle and how the development lifecycle compliments this

. . .

The following is a set of criteria for a Project Manager;

• 5 years experience as a Project Manager working on software projects

• A broad understanding of technology

• Strong leadership and project management capabilities

• Ideally experienced in managing projects within your market or vertical

• Exceptional time management abilities

• Experience being involved in and managing multiple projects

• Experience with the development lifecycle

• Exceptional reporting and written communication skills

Questions

Because you may not understand the CTO role's technical aspects, you will rely on the resume they put forward and references you contact to confirm their experience.

• Tell me a little about yourself? What do you like to do on the weekends?

• Tell me your favorite project to date and why?

• When do you know the project is off track?

• If the project is off schedule, how do you get it back on track?

• Describe a process for managing technology budgets

- Have you managed remote teams and outsourced resources before? If so, describe the challenges you faced
- How do you manage a team or an individual that is not performing to their full potential?
- Describe how you keep all stakeholders of a project informed
- Explain your process for delegation
- What's the biggest mistake you've made in your career, and how did you go about remedying it
- How do you prioritize tasks?
- How familiar are you with agile methodologies? Describe what Agile is.
- How would you design a company's technology strategy?
- What technologies are you experienced with?
- Do you know how to read and write code?
- If I asked for a daily/weekly report on development progress, explain in detail what you would provide me with.

You can ask similar questions of a Project Manager with the exception of the ones relating to technology strategy and development. The main thing you're looking for in a Project Manager is their ability to keep the project on track and give you honest and open feedback.

- Tell me a little about yourself? What do you like to do on the weekends?
- Tell me your favorite project to date and why?

- When do you know the project is off track?
- If the project is off schedule, how do you get it back on track?
- Describe a process for managing project budgets
- Have you managed remote teams and outsourced resources before? If so, describe the challenges you faced
- How do you manage a team or an individual that is not working to their full potential?
- Describe how you keep all stakeholders of a project informed
- Explain your process for delegation
- What's the biggest mistake you've made on a project, and how did you go about remedying it
- How do you prioritize project tasks?
- What project management software do you prefer?
- What project management methodologies are you skilled at?
- If I asked for a daily/weekly report on development progress, explain in detail what you would provide me with.
- You've been asked to manage a project where the development resources are all part of an external agency. What cadences and processes do you put in place to ensure the project runs smoothly and with complete transparency?

Summary

If you want to get your software built up to the point of being commercially viable, then an agency is an excellent choice as it allows you to focus entirely on building your business and have zero concern about your technology. If you have established software that someone else created, an agency might also be a good choice, or perhaps it would be better to employ your own full-time developers to build out the new features you have in the pipeline. If you have your own team and need support, again, an agency might be a good choice, or you might utilize external contractors instead, or a blend of the two. It entirely depends on several factors, including your development stage, budget, time demand, type of application, release structure (are you releasing new features all the time), and quality of pre-existing software. May you may also choose to work with an agency indefinitely and never employ your own full-time developers.

The ultimate decision on who you're going to get to work on your software is one you need to make yourself. But it does make sense to use an experienced agency when you're starting from scratch as you remove all of the overheads of running your own internal team. If you are delivering new features all the time, then you will find employing full-time developers will work out more cost-effective in the long run. I would suggest only using contractors if you have deep pockets and need to fill a missing skillset for a short period of time. Even as a skilled developer taking on the role of CTO in a startup, partnering with an agency will get your software to market faster without the full-time overheads.

. . .

Remember, a development team consists of more than just developers. You need to ensure you have the accompanying team members to ensure your software will be successful.

Protecting Your IP

Protecting your Intellectual Property (IP) is very important, and you should take steps to ensure whoever is developing your application is bound by both confidentiality and intellectual property protection. I need to state that nothing in this section constitutes legal advice, and you should always speak to your legal counsel. If you're signing a contract provided by an agency, I recommend having your attorney look over it first.

Most reputable development agencies will have well-structured legal contracts they will ask you to enter into, but you may also seek to use your own provided by your attorney. Most agencies won't like you using your own as they will need to have their legal team look over it, and it delays the whole onboarding process (and the cost of this will be added to your build). Some agencies will refuse to sign anything but their own. In addition, they've likely already spent $ 10,000's on their contracts, and if they're reputable, they honestly don't want your IP. If you're using contractors or are going down the full-time employment path, however, you will need your own employment contract for them to sign. Whether you're signing an agency's contract or having your legal council produce one, the two most important clauses are your confidentiality clause and your intellectual property clause.

So what's the difference between confidentiality and intellectual property? Confidentiality refers to the disclosure of any information that the provider of that information considers to be confidential. Generally, this is in the form of written or verbal communications or documents. On the other hand, intellectual property (IP) is the property of your mind or proprietary knowledge. It can be an invention, trademark, design, brand, or the application of your idea (your software). Simply put, your idea is your IP, and so is the resulting app or software produced from it.

Confidentiality

Confidentiality is about ensuring anyone who works on your project or reads your build bible is bound by confidentiality and cannot **share** the information (IP) with anyone. The most common clauses will state the information is confidential until you make that information public. In most business-to-business scenarios, confidentiality is mutual. That is, they promise to keep your information confidential, and you promise to keep their information confidential. Sometimes confidentiality clauses will also discuss how information is stored and may put restrictions on where and how you can store any confidential information. As a general rule, if your idea is unique, you should have someone sign a confidentiality agreement ***BEFORE*** you start discussing it with them. Otherwise, legally, anything you've told them before you execute a deed of confidentiality will technically fall outside its protection. In some circumstances, this is not always true but remember, your information is your IP. So take steps to protect it.

Intellectual Property

Intellectual Property clauses, on the other hand, are designed to protect the **use** of your IP. This means while confidentiality is about the disclosure of your IP, actual IP clauses protect you against any unauthorized use. While this is not foolproof, a super simple and cost-effective way to help protect your IP is to snail mail yourself or your attorney a copy of your build bible and ***NEVER*** open the envelope. When you mail it, your idea essentially has a date stamp on it, so if anyone says they had the idea first, they need to prove it was before this date. Again, this is not legal advice and certainly not airtight in a court of law but can offer some protection if you don't have a legal document with someone.

An IP clause needs to state that ***YOU*** will own the right to *ALL* IP produced during the engagement with a developer. It may also say that they will grant you a non-exclusive and royalty-free right to use any of their IP that existed before the engagement if it is a part of your application. These days, it's entirely normal for developers to use libraries they've developed over and over again to save time. In addition, developers use a lot of third-party libraries when building software as well. These all have non-exclusive royalty-free use. So ultimately, the IP clause is protecting your idea and anything **newly** created during the time the developer was engaged.

. . .

The key takeaway is to make sure the IP clause states that you will own your IP and make sure it's in a legally binding document signed by both parties.

The final thing I will leave you within this section is a word of warning regarding jurisdiction. Jurisdiction refers to the court responsible for upholding and ruling on any breach of the clauses in a contract. Be very careful dealing with offshore development agencies that do not have a **committed legal presence** in your country. Asking a company that doesn't have a **committed legal presence** in your country to sign an agreement is almost a waste of time if anything goes wrong. For example, if you're in the US and dealing with a development company outside of the states (South East Asia or South America, for example), you may not have the protection the document is designed to offer.

In most cases, this is different if you're dealing with a hybrid agency with a committed presence (i.e., registered companies) in the US and overseas. The reason is that the US company you're dealing with is bound by US law, and they are the entity signing the contract.

However, as I've already mentioned, if you pick a reputable agency, you should avoid all of the issues highlighted in this section.

5

CREATE A CLICKABLE PROTOTYPE

Sadly, number 5 is the one that always gets forgotten but is easily the difference between an app that kills it or one that struggles to gain traction. The art of the clickable prototype isn't new. It's been around for more than a decade. But astonishingly, only a small number of apps create a clickable prototype before cutting a line of code. This is especially true for anyone building an app with a development agency or third party. It's probably why most apps don't get any traction in a reasonable amount of time, as this is where all software begins its life.

I like to think of the Clickable Prototype as your 'idea' insurance policy. It helps you quickly validate whether your idea solves a customers' problem, and I strongly recommend you don't skip this crucial step. It also enables you to find flaws in your UX/UI that could improve app engagement exponentially, meaning your average screen time just doubled. So what is a clickable prototype?

. . .

A clickable prototype is a 'dummy' version of your app's core features with a fully designed and functional User Interface. It doesn't have any 'brains' or 'smarts,' but it acts and feels like it's real. You can click around your app and flow to different views and perform a predefined set of user flows and functions.

The clickable prototype starts with wireframing, which essentially focuses on layout and User Experience (UX). It then moves on to taking the wireframes and turning them into static views or screens by designing a User Interface (UI) based on your brand and color theme. A good analogy would be going to an architect to design your dream home. They start by drawing up the plans that are in black and white and flat. These plans describe where your rooms are and how you would flow through your home. Once they **validate** your design and get **feedback** from you, they then create mockups of facades and 3d renders of the interior and exterior to get a better feel for how it will look when built. And at every step of the way, you can make changes.

Creating a clickable prototype is very similar. You start with the black and white wireframe and understand how a user will flow through the application and where all the elements should be positioned on the page/view. Below I've included some examples of wireframes and the stages they will typically go through.

Most wireframes start like this;

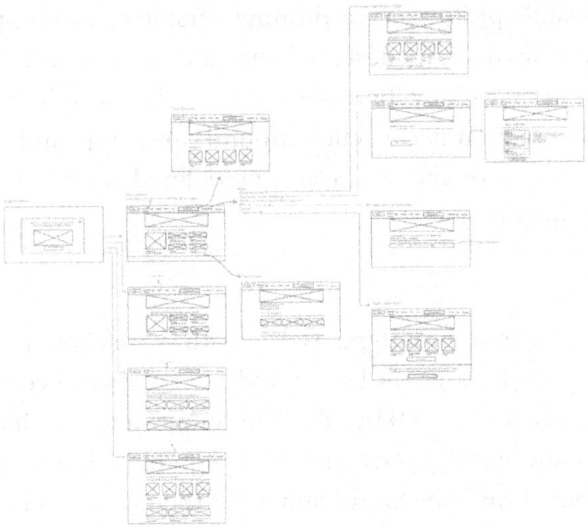

Hand Drawn Wireframes - Image Credit InVision https://www.invisionapp.com/inside-design/wireframe-examples/

And end up like this;

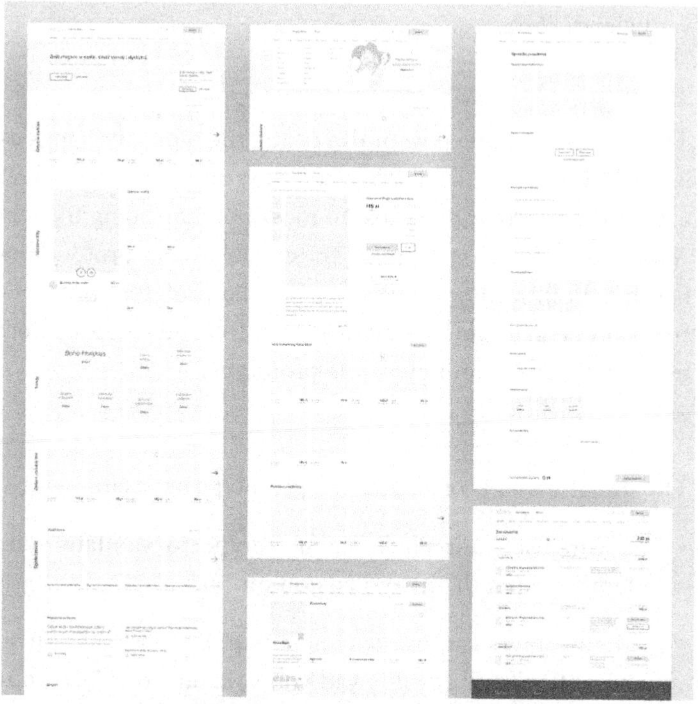

Completed Wireframes - Image Credit InVision https://www.invisionapp.com/inside-design/wireframe-examples/

As you can see, they transition from rough sketches to more detailed layouts. These layouts are also clickable, but they're not usually shared with customers at this stage.

You then take these black and white images and turn them into color and add all the final product details. This creates your User Interface and shows you exactly how your app will look when it's finished. The last piece of the puzzle is then to create links between all the elements in the UI so you can touch buttons etc., and they take you to their relevant views.

The actual clickable part of the prototype typically happens in a third-party piece of software. Most designers these days use a design program, with the most popular being Sketch, Adobe InDesign, or Figma. These tools have prototyping features built-in, but another incredible prototyping tool is InVision which works well with Sketch and allows direct user feedback on your clickable prototype.

The major benefits of a clickable prototype are as follows;

- You can use your clickable prototype to validate your problem statement with real customers
- Real customers can use it almost like it was a real app so you know feedback is valid and you validate your UX (your users can find things and flow through the app how you expect)
- Your idea is now tangible, and you can use it to demonstrate to investors
- You get a feel for how your app will look and function once built
- You can extend your clickable prototype to include future features that won't exist in your first release
- You can save thousands of dollars in rework and redevelopment by validating your assumptions and user experience before cutting a line of code

. . .

All highly successful apps prototype, so why would you skip this crucial step when working with an agency? Firstly, most agencies don't prototype because it's an extra cost they need to sell, and it can sometimes mean pausing development. Additionally, most clients don't realize the benefits of prototyping, so they might think the agency is trying to upsell them, or the process will consume part of their development budget. The reality is your agency or team will need to do most of this work anyway. They need to create the wireframes and the UI before the developers start cutting code. While developers are intelligent people, they're not all that imaginative, and the UI is part of helping them visualize what they're building. So the UI needs to be designed before any development begins, and a good agency will wireframe first and validate it with you.

The extra cost to turn the UI into a clickable prototype is only 2-3 days plus maybe a week for you to spend time getting feedback from customers. Finally, there may be another 1-2 days making any tweaks or changes based on user feedback. So for around a week of extra cost and a week of validation time, you may very well save yourself tens or even hundreds of thousands of dollars! Kind of worth it, wouldn't you agree?

"I like to think of the Clickable Prototype as your 'idea' insurance policy."

. . .

Ok, so now that you understand the importance of a clickable prototype and it won't cost you a considerable amount of budget, we can move on to the next step to gain customer validation.

6

CUSTOMER VALIDATION

Through this book, we've been taking steps to gain more and more clarity and generate many assumptions about our customer segment and how they might interact and flow through our application. We've made assumptions about what features they would prioritize over others and what would help you win them over any competitors. It's now time to validate most if not all of these assumptions.

Before we dive into the process, I want to make you aware that customer validation and refinement should never end. You should constantly be striving to make your app better and better and validating changes along the way. If you stop validating, it means you've stopped innovating and listening to your users, and there's only one way that will go.

Earlier on, we spoke about creating an assumptions register which is simply a list of all the assumptions we've made up until this point. The idea behind the register is to remind you that you made these assumptions and record whether they are valid or invalid. Your assumptions register is such a powerful tool as it makes sure you're backing up and reinforcing your beliefs along with checking in to make sure they're still accurate. But even more critical than this, you're ensuring your app is always something your users want, need, and can't live without by constantly innovating.

The validation process is as simple as confirming assumption A is valid and assumption B is invalid and documenting this in your register. Just as in our story card writing, it is imperative to include the 'Why' or the 'reason' your assumption was proven valid or invalid. The complicated part in all of this is the proving part. Just like a detective on a crime scene, you need real tangible evidence to back up your finding. Otherwise, the judge isn't going to rule on a determination. So the 'Why' is both the reason and part of the evidence.

How you gather your evidence will depend entirely on the particular assumption you're looking to prove, but the key is to start gathering evidence before the crime is even committed. Every app and every idea will be different, so I cannot give you a comprehensive list of specific validation points, but I can give you a process I use that works in 99% of cases. The general rule is to gather evidence early and gather it often. Once you have enough evidence, then and only then, do you make a ruling.

Validation Process

The process begins when you make an assumption about your business, product, app, user, and anything in between. Some assumptions will have a minor to zero impact on your business, while others can sink you overnight. It would be best if you used common sense as to what goes on the register, but anything that will impact your bottom line should be recorded as a general rule.

The way I suggest you run your assumptions register is by grouping your assumptions into common categories. You should then set up different processes for gathering and storing evidence for each of the sub-categories and have a set time each week that you review the evidence and decide if you can pass judgment or not. Let's look at an example;

For Customer Validation, create a category called Customer (I call mine Customer Success), and under this, add the following sub-categories;

- Customer Demographics
- Customer Motivations
- Customer Goals
- Customer Pains
- Customer Channels
- Customer Deal Makers
- Customer Deal Breakers

- Customer Feature & Priority
- Customer Price Point
- Customer UX
- Customer Branding Acceptance

These are all valid assumption sub-categories that should go on your register, and all can have a significant impact on your bottom line. Can you see that these categories validate and monitor the assumptions made in Chapter 1 in the Customer Persona and some made in Chapter 2? The next step is to implement several means of gathering evidence to prove or disprove the assumptions you've made under each of the sub-categories. You can collect this evidence from the following sources;

- Marketing Feedback
- Surveys
- Analytics & Tracking
- Ad Analytics & Tracking
- App Analytics & UX Tracking
- A/B Tests
- Recorded or Documented Customer Interviews
- Customer Support Monitoring & Feedback

Almost all of the data collection can be automated, so you're not manually scrambling to collect the evidence. Each week you should schedule a time to review the data and make your ruling. I plan a time each Thursday to run a report using a combination of my marketing software and support software to check if the evidence for my assumptions stacks up. Even if I have already validated any of these sub-categories, I always check to ensure the proof still stacks up, and so should you.

You see the market moves and shifts. It's never stationary. So thinking of your Customer assumptions as stationary will see your attrition rates rise over time. In fact, thinking of any of your categories as fixed is very dangerous. By assessing and reassessing constantly, you're protecting your existing customer base, refining how to obtain new customers (growing your customer base), and garnishing intelligence of potential new markets.

If you have more than one Customer Segment, you should have a sub-category for each as you would have made slightly different assumptions about each. Their demographics and motivations for using your product might be very different, and their features and priorities may also be very different. The critical takeaway is to have a sub-category of assumptions for each customer segment within a product.

While this chapter is specifically about Customer Validation, it's worth mentioning I use the assumptions register for my entire business. As an example, another category I have is the Revenue Vault. My Revenue Vault contains all the assumptions I have about my revenue streams and revenue models, including assumptions relating to the source of the revenue. Like my Customer Success sub-categories, I collect and monitor all of the data related to my product revenues. Note that I said Product and not Business. Of course have data collection and monitoring concerning my business revenue, but because I have more than one product line, this data is an aggregate of all revenue streams. The critical difference is the business revenue provides evidence as to the health of my business as a ***whole.*** *In contrast, the* product revenue offers data on the health of that specific product line. By separating the two, I can effortlessly identify a failing or mediocre product long before it becomes a negative cost center. If I only focussed on the business sub-category and ignored the individual product, I run the risk of not making the business as successful and profitable as I can. Or worse, my business failing because I didn't see a product line was destroying profits. If you have more than one product line, I suggest you do the same.

The process for creating your assumptions register is a simple six-step process;

1. create your core categories,

2. break these up into sensible sub-categories,

3. capture your key assumptions under each,

4. collect the evidence (automate this as much as possible),

5. when you've collected enough evidence, pass judgment (valid or invalid),

6. assess and reassess

Every business and product is different, so I can't give you the perfect list of categories and sub-categories. However, the Customer sub-categories above are a great starting point for your software. For a little further insight, the top 5 I use to monitor the health of my business overall are;

1. Customer Success

2. Revenue Vault

3. Cost Defence

4. Product Power

5. Business Gladiator

I know these have funky names, and you can call your categories and sub-categories whatever you like. But have fun with it and make them meaningful to you. You'll be more empowered by your categories if you give them meaningful titles.

The key takeaway I want you to have from this chapter is that you will make assumptions about your Customer and your business every day. You must constantly collect evidence and validate and re-validate these assumptions to ensure your customers become raving fans. Raving fan customers are sticky customers, and they're the best kind. You will spend significant amounts to acquire your Customer, so the longer you keep them, the greater your return on investment and the greater your customers' lifetime value.

Every app has the potential to be successful. Those that record, validate and reassess their core customer assumptions are the ones that become market leaders.

7

ADHERE TO STRICT AGILE DEVELOPMENT PRATICE

Agile methodologies have been around since early 2001 when 17 people met to discuss the future of developing software in the modern era. Their frustrations ran deep with software being created as if you were building a house or manufacturing a car where everything was planned upfront and made and released in a big bang approach. This created massive budget overruns and software that no longer met the need it was initially intended for because the users' problem had changed (these projects typically took 1-2 years to complete). Or worse, the software didn't work at all. This approach in project management terms is called 'waterfall'.

After an extended weekend of debate, the Agile Manifesto of just 68 words emerged and has changed software development forever. The manifesto describes the four fundamental values of agile, and while new technologies and platforms emerge, these four values still hold significant weight today.

* * *

Manifesto for Agile Software Development

We are uncovering better ways of developing software by doing it and helping others do it.

Through this work we have come to value:

Individuals and interactions over processes and tools

Working software over comprehensive documentation

Customer collaboration over contract negotiation

Responding to change over following a plan

That is, while there is value in the items on the right, we value the items on the left more.

* * *

The 17 people responsible for this manifesto are;

1. Kent Beck

2. Mike Beedle

3. Arie van Bennekum

4. Alistair Cockburn

5. Ward Cunningham

6. Martin Fowler

7. James Grenning

8. Jim Highsmith

9. Andrew Hunt

10. Ron Jefferies

11. Jon Kern

12. Brian Marick

13. Robert C. Martin

14. Steve Mellor

15. Ken Schwaber

16. Jeff Sutherland

17. Dave Thomas

The creators of the manifesto also produced 12 principles. From these, several agile methodologies were born to deliver on the values and principles of what agile promised.

I've spent a couple of pages explaining all of this because you must understand when talking to developers, there isn't just one form of agile. So asking an agency or developer do you do agile can mean many different things.

However, on its base level, Agile refers to an iterative style of development where teams program software in small increments. It focuses on **continuous delivery** and constantly seeks and **values** customer feedback. In agile terms, an increment will generally be referred to as a sprint. A sprint can be anywhere from 1-8 weeks in length, but most are no more than two weeks. The idea is that at the end of each sprint, the team should have a 'shippable' piece of software. Therefore, after the sprint, it should be possible to push a new feature or function live to customers.

For small teams like those that would most likely be building your software, Scrum is the preferred agile methodology to follow. Scrum is a methodology where work is done in short sprints of usually 2-4 weeks. Every day the team meets at a scheduled time for 10-15mins and completes a standup. A standup is an opportunity for each team member to discuss the work they did yesterday, what they're doing today, and if they have any issues or things preventing (blocking) them from completing their allocated story cards. It's also an opportunity for the developers to ask the Product Owner to clarify any of the stories or ask questions. The whole scrum framework helps teams work together and encourages them to learn through experiences, self-organize, and reflect on their wins and losses, all while striving to improve continuously.

You'll note some of this will be sounding familiar as I've mentioned parts of the Scrum methodology throughout this book. In chapter 4, I said one of the requirements you should have of an agency is a daily meeting of 10-15mins where the developers are present. This meeting not only lets you see there is constant progress on your software but also allows the developer to ask you (the Product Owner) any questions they might have about a particular feature they're developing. In chapter 2, we learned how to write story cards and the value of their simple yet powerful construct (although story cards are not unique to Scrum).

The Product Owner (you) is responsible for the priorities in the backlog and can change these priorities at any time. You're responsible for clarifying the features and making sure the features are what the customer wants. If working with an agency, be careful when moving priorities mid-development as this can start to cause budget overrun. Try to swap features that take the same amount of effort to develop where possible.

I'm not going to go any deeper in discussing the mechanics or details of Scrum or agile. What I wanted to achieve from this chapter is that you understand what agile is and why it's essential for your project. I also wanted you to get a sense of how an agile team should operate so you can make sure your developers or agency are following these principles. If they're not following these principles, it will be costing you money and therefore wasted development budget.

The key takeaways from this chapter should be to insist your developers or agency adhere to strict agile practices. As the Product Owner, you want to be a part of their daily standup, have the final say on your backlog, and are responsible for the priorities within.

CONCLUSION

We've covered a lot in this book, and as you can see, I'm deeply passionate about the Appiphany™ process. And that's because when you get this right and implement this process, you get your fantastic idea built for less and see your business skyrocket.

With the information in this book, you have everything you need to get out there and create killer apps for less cost that obliterate competitors and draw users to them like a magnet. However, if you would like to just have OpsGuard™ do it for you, and you're serious about getting the best outcome possible while dominating your market and maximizing user growth, for a limited time, we're offering you a 30-minute strategy session where we'll discuss your idea, business goals and challenges and present the entire Appiphany™ process for you for free.

Please note this is NOT a sales call. You will be speaking with one of our highly experienced Technology Strategists, not a salesman.

Warning: Before you claim your free strategy session, you must understand that this is only for people serious about setting up their app and business for long-term success. We'll do the brunt of the work, but to truly get your app to skyrocket, we need your commitment and dedication to the Appiphany™ process.

But if you are ready to kick your success into overdrive and understand your apps' potential, book your FREE strategy session by following the below link now.

I recommend you book quickly. Our Technology Strategists only have a limited number of slots available for free sessions each month, and they're filling up fast. You may also be lucky enough to get your session booked with me directly. Go ahead and lock it in now https://meeting.opsguard.io/meetings/opsteam/30min-ceo-strategy-session

Thank you for taking the time to read this book. I know the information contained within will be invaluable, and I know the process works, having proved it on 100s of successful software builds. I can't wait to speak to you in person or hear how Appiphany™ guided your success.

. . .

To your unlimited success,

Kerry Esson

appiphany@opsguard.io

ABOUT THE AUTHOR

Kerry Esson is a seasoned entrepreneur, business owner, technology coach, and startup mentor. He is regarded as one of the foremost authorities on technology business mastery, having built and exited several successful tech startups. With more than 20 years of business and technology experience, Kerry has been involved in and personally built 100s of successful software projects for his own companies, startups, and enterprises alike. Kerry teaches the tools and strategies to make more revenue and garnish more users, but more importantly, develop exceptional ideas into reality via the most cost-effective and efficient means possible.

Kerry is an expert at helping business owners turn their software idea into highly profitable user acquisition machines. In Kerry's Appiphany™ workshops, he teaches the detailed strategies you can implement even in today's economy to ensure your revenues, users, and profits soar.

That's the premise Appiphany™ was built upon and the blueprint for wildly successful software.